Unhindered

THE SEVEN ESSENTIAL PRACTICES FOR **OVERCOMING INSECURITY**

JAEMIN FRAZER

UNHINDERED. THE SEVEN ESSENTIAL PRACTICES
FOR OVERCOMING INSECURITY.

National Library of Australia Cataloguing-in-Publication entry:

Frazer, Jaemin, author.
Unhindered. The Seven Essential Practices for Overcoming Insecurity /
Jaemin Frazer.
ISBN: 978-0-6488942-0-9 (paperback)
Self Help
Mind Body

Contents

Preface

For the last ten years, the pursuit of solving the insecurity problem has become my obsession. It has entirely captured my attention and all ambition I have for my life is directed to this end.

This subject has occupied every spare corner of my brain and there are very few nights where the desire to understand and explain how insecurity can be overcome does not work itself into the fabric of my dreams.

This book represents the very best I have to offer on this subject. I have poured my heart and soul into creating a framework that is intelligent, effective and complete.

To set up the conversation about such a difficult and vulnerable issue, there are three vital distinctions to be made about the nature of insecurity:

1. It is natural
2. It is useful
3. It is removable

In understanding this triad, you will find the access point into the way of solving insecurity for good.

It is natural

It is unavoidable. Even perfect parents could not protect their children from developing irrational fears and self-limiting beliefs. Doubt and fear show us where the edges are. They let us know we are alive and that we deserve to be safe.

It is universal. Every human being who has ever lived, and is yet to live, will face this same longing for love, belonging and significance in the process of forming as an adult. Understanding the universal nature of the fear of not being good enough allows each of us to see our own struggle with insecurity as somehow special or unique. It's not that some people face the insecurity problem while others are spared, everyone develops this fear. If insecurity is the constant, the variable is what people do with it.

It is useful

There are seasons of life where having something to prove, driven by fear is incredibly motivating. In this book, I'll show you examples of insecurity driving up performance and boosting personal capabilities.

The issue is that while it starts out as natural and useful, there is definitely an expiry date on both the usefulness and naturality of this fear. In fact, the longer insecurity remains intact and unaddressed inside you, the more toxic and maddening it becomes. We are supposed to remove it.

The gift within our insecurity is the resistance it provides. Growth never exists in a vacuum or perfect condition. It requires some kind of oppositional force. We reach full stature as we reach for the stars while simultaneously being pulled back to earth. If there was no gravity, we would float off into space.

From the deep dark recesses of our mind a voice of fear taunts us. The terrifying question of what would be discovered if we were to be laid bare, can either paralyse or energise us.

What if it's true? What if you are no good? What if you are unworthy? What if you are not enough?

*Sure, but what if it's **not** true? What if there is no substance to this fear? What if I am inherently good? What if I am deeply worthy? What if I AM enough?*

The voice of insecurity gives us the opportunity to find out which one is true. The most meaningful victories in life always come in the face of the biggest challenges.

Insecurity proves to be a worthy adversary to test yourself against. Like a loving mentor, it desperately wants you to win while making it as difficult as possible for you to do so. This makes the victory real.

Nothing of value comes without a cost. To have the opportunity to genuinely overcome insecurity will cost you everything. If you lose, you die. If you win, you get the holy grail and are able to drink from the well of everlasting life.

It is removable

I have no confidence in the common thinking about what one is to do with self-doubt, fear and limiting beliefs. The advice of podcasters, authors and athletes on dealing with fear frequently leaves me puzzled, while conversations about insecurity with practitioners in the personal development space rarely inspire me.

The general consensus seems to be to struggle against insecurity the best you can. Mask, medicate and manage the monster. It is my heartfelt conviction that we can and must do better than that. The natural cycle of insecurity is for it to be felt, faced, deconstructed, removed and replaced.

This book is devoted to the process of *solving* the insecurity problem.

Jaemin

Introduction

So, what's the problem?

Let me begin with 2 of my all-time favourite coaching questions:

1. What problem are you most looking to solve right now?
2. Are you sure that's really the problem?

Two interesting things happen when you allow these questions to work their magic.

Firstly, most people realise that they've never actually named the problem. They are not actually clear about what's wrong at all. This question forces you to be specific. What exactly is the problem here? You can't fix it if you don't even know what it is. What exactly is wrong? What specifically don't you like?

Being as precise as possible gives you clarity about where to focus your attention in order to fix the problem.

Maybe your marriage isn't great right now.

Is it everything about your marriage or only certain parts of your marriage? What's not the way you want it to be?

Maybe you haven't felt healthy in ages.

Yes, but what specifically is happening in your body that makes you feel unhealthy?

Perhaps your finances are stressing you out.

What do you mean by that?

Maybe you feel stuck or trapped and haven't been happy in ages.

Are you sure that's how you feel? And how do you know this is true?

Or maybe every time you arrive at work, there is an empty feeling in the pit if your stomach.

What exactly is the problem here?

When you remain vague or abstract about the things that aren't working, you have no capacity to improve your situation.

Secondly, just because you think you've accurately understood the problem doesn't mean to say that you have. Because problems feel bad, they almost always come with an inbuilt sense of judgment. We feel that we must have done something wrong to be experiencing this problem in the first place. And if you've done something wrong, there must BE something wrong with you. It all becomes very personal.

The pain associated with this problem makes it incredibly hard to clearly see the true nature of the problem itself. It is impossible to do self-judgment and self-awareness at the same time. In the presence of judgment, we must defend and protect our interests instead. This invariably leads to a faulty diagnosis.

We see and feel pain on the surface and therefore imagine that's where the problem lies. Due to our inadequate diagnosis though, we waste effort solving the things that are merely symptoms of a deeper problem. This leaves us in more pain and more deeply impacted by the underlying problem.

Be precise

The value of letting these two questions do their work is that you move from abstraction to specificity. Embedded in this shift is the experience of moving from powerlessness to full empowerment.

When a problem is experienced in loose, abstract and imprecise language, you'll notice that the problem appears to be outside of you in a way that you have zero control over. The accompanying feeling is therefore to be overwhelmed and anxious. There is nothing you can really do to solve the problem; you'll just need to manage the situation as best you can.

As you get precise and accurately identify the real problem, however, you'll notice that it is actually entirely within your aegis. You are therefore completely capable of solving the problem. The feeling about the problem changes significantly. As soon as you see clearly the exact nature of the problem, you also see that the problem is you. You discover that the problem is not due to what is happening to you, as first thought, but what you are bringing to the situation.

When you feel overwhelmed and anxious about a problem, this is simply clean feedback to let you know that you haven't properly understood what the real problem is. You will know that you've accurately understood the true problem when you feel clear about the solution and confident that you are capable of resolving the issue.

Let's try this idea in the five most common human pain points.

Weird Health Stuff

Amanda's story – Health pain

For a number of years, Amanda had experienced increasingly serious health issues, to the point of being severely limited by her medical conditions. Things just kept getting worse and her life had practically ground to a halt. The physical sickness was ruining her business and relationships. Therefore, when she came to see me, the problem she was most looking to solve, was the negative impact her health was having on every area of her life.

Now obviously I'm no doctor, but that was kind of the point. She had already spent thousands of dollars on numerous medical specialists and none of them had been able to give her more than vague diagnoses and generalised ways of managing her health. The value of asking me to observe her situation was that because I was not impacted by her pain, and had no vested interest in solving her problem, I was able to see patterns that were hidden to those closer to the situation.

Here is what emerged after some gentle inquiry:

- She had always been very healthy until a few years into starting her own business,
- Over the last 5 years, she got really sick twice a year and each time was worse than the one before,
- Being sick forced her to be cared for by her mum,
- She described herself as a chronic people pleaser and could never say no.

Exploring the unconscious strategies beneath these patterns it became apparent that:

- Because her dreams were not initially supported by her parents, as many young people do, she made a vow to prove them wrong.
- While this driven-ness caused her to be highly motivated and achieve some remarkable results it was also a brutal strategy with zero scope for intentional rest. Becoming really sick was the only time she stopped.
- Being sick was the only time her mother and her knew how to do relationship naturally. Mum would take charge and care for her little girl. They'd never worked out how to do adult to adult relationship even though Amanda was in her 30's and had lived out of home for more than 15 years. There was certainty and safety in this set up that unconsciously caused them both to hang onto the sick-ness because of the relationship benefits.
- Being a people pleaser means always saying yes and

serving other people's agenda even at your own expense. Being bed ridden provided the only opportunity for saying no without feeling guilty.

Clearly, the problem actually had nothing to do with health. Every time she had focused on solving the health problem before only ever led to short-term benefits and actually added residual disappointment.

The real problem needing to be solved here was entirely about her sense of self. A deep insecurity had been undermining her independence, assertiveness and adult decision making. Her ill health was simply the by-product of this dysfunction.

Robbie's story – Losing weight

Robbie came to me looking to achieve three outcomes, one of which was to lose 15 kilograms. He'd been trying hard to get his weight under control for most of his adult life. Fifteen years ago, he successfully lost 20 kgs but didn't manage to keep it off and has been overweight ever since despite his best attempts at diet and exercise.

Robbie thought that his problem was he'd never liked fruit and didn't enjoy exercise. He felt that he just lacked the discipline and consistency to stick to a health plan that would enable him to lose the weight.

I was far less convinced this had anything to do with the extra kilos. Being curious about what had created this issue in the first place led us to discover the real problem.

The breakthrough came when I asked him if it was ok for him to be attractive. He laughed. No one had ever called him attractive, and he'd never thought that of himself. He'd been the happy, friendly, cuddly teddy bear for as long as he could remember.

The thing is, when Robbie was 10 years old, he had a particularly painful experience at his school athletics carnival. He'd decided that this would be the year he would emerge as talented young athlete and so had convinced his dad to buy him some flash new running spikes along with a matching pair of shorts and racing singlet. On top of this, he confidently told his friends and classmates that he'd hoped to win some or all of the races.

Unfortunately, on the day of the carnival things didn't go to plan and he failed to even win a ribbon of any colour, new spikes and all. His mates took great pleasure in reminding him of this fact and made fun of him mercilessly.

When I took him back to that defining moment to review the data, Robbie realised that the impact of that experience had changed his whole life. Specifically, it was the meaning he'd placed on that event that really defined him.

In that moment Robbie decided that when you stand out, you get found out.

See Robbie thought he had a weight issue, a motivation problem, and a fruit problem. The truth is, that he's been hiding since he was 10! This is clearly not a health problem. This is about insecurity.

Losing weight and being attractive is incredibly dangerous because it would bring him face to face with his deepest fear – being found out!

Until he deals with this insecurity, there is no possible way his subconscious will allow him to lose weight. It will use all kinds of fun but untrue stories to keep him in the dark about what is really going on.

Erica's story – Extra weight

At 40, Erica was really sick of the way she looked. The extra 15 kilos of weight she'd been carrying was creating massive pain and although she'd done everything she could think of to try and fix it, she was desperate to resolve this issue for good.

As you'll see later in the book, feeling acute pain about what you don't want is incredibly useful for real change. In the safety of a clean judgement free coaching space, we were able to explore the issue more deeply.

Erica imagined that the real problem was that she lacked the discipline and motivation to stay on track with a diet and exercise regime. She explained that she was not naturally drawn to sport, fitness or exercise and so always had to force myself to do these things. As a busy working mother, these things kept getting pushed down the list of priorities.

She also told me that her mum always solved relationship problems with food and that is exactly what she has learnt to do as well.

I told her that this was not the problem but that clearly, she needed to be fat.

After she got over the initial shock caused by the brutality of that assessment, we both roared with laughter! What other space could I say those words to a woman without getting stabbed in the throat with a fork?

I explained that I didn't care whether she was skinny or fat. It made no difference to me! She told me she wanted to be skinny yet was constantly unable to achieve that result despite her best efforts. The point is that obviously, this is not about better diet and exercise otherwise she would have already worked out how to solve that problem.

There must be a deeper problem to solve before she can see change in the issue with her health.

I began exploring the deeper issue by asking if she had always been unhappy with her weight. Here's what we discovered:

- It was only 15 years ago that her weight had increased. Before that, she had never had a problem with staying healthy.
- Things changed after her fiancé cheated on her in the lead up to their wedding, when she was at her most slim and attractive. From that point, weight had been an issue.
- She'd attached her whole hope for happiness, family, and security on this relationship and couldn't imagine a life without him, so she continued with the marriage and suppressed the pain of being hurt so personally.
- Once she was married to him, her deep fear was that he would reject her again. That would prove once and for all that she was not good enough.
- The unconscious protection strategy to keep herself safe from this fear therefore was to never show up at her best again. That way, if he was to cheat on her again, he'd be rejecting the fat her, not the real her.

Clearly Erica does not have a weight issue.

Having an extra 15 kilograms was allowing her to hide from what she was most afraid of. Therefore, it was not safe for her to lose the weight without first dealing with the deep insecurity.

Bernadette's story – Super skinny

Bernadette was obsessed with being skinny and looking good. She didn't look like she had an eating disorder and boasted that she ate a cheeseburger everyday. She wasn't anorexic or bulimic. She looked perfectly fit and well. It wasn't until she was pregnant with her first baby and the thought of being 'big' compromised not only her own health but her baby's health as well. She came to me because her friends and family were worried about her and because she was suffering severe anxiety about not being fit and skinny.

Here's what we discovered:

- She grew up in a large family. Her dad would favour the pretty, skinny daughters as opposed to the larger, less pretty ones
- Her parents later divorced
- She connected skinny and attractive with not being rejected
- She was highly motivated to stay skinny so her husband wouldn't leave her
- She thrived on the compliments she'd get, and this measured her value and worth
- As a result, she created an arbitrary number on the scales she could never let herself exceed.
- She never missed an exercise session, even when it cost her in other ways

- Has been on every diet under the sun — no sugar, keto, 5-2, eat only a handful, etc

While it is much easier to judge people who are overweight, the point is, some skinny people are just as insecure. They are driven to not get fat out of a fear of rejection, a need to be affirmed or a craving for attention. Ultimately however, they are still hiding from being found out, just in a different way. The deep fear is that if they were to show up as themselves, there would be nothing special about them and they would be exposed.

The point is, this was clearly not a health issue, a weight issue or even an anxiety issue for Bernadette. This all came back to her fear that she was not really worthy of love.

Weird health stuff

I geek out on health conditions that doctors are at a loss to know what to do with. The moment someone describes their condition this way, I'm super curious to explore the real problem.

You've got psoriasis...there is no cure. You'll have that for the rest of your life and need to constantly treat the symptoms.

Autoimmune diseases. Sorry...got nothing. Just get some rest and try to avoid stressful situations.

Suddenly developed bad allergies to certain foods and

additives...steer clear of nuts, eggs, gluten, soap, sugar and carry an EpiPen at all times!

If it's a weird health thing, then more than likely it's actually not weird at all. Calling it weird is only making it more powerful and giving you less ability to do anything about it. What if it is simply the symptom of a deeper problem?

People work perfectly. You are not broken. The results you are getting in every area of life are the exact results you've designed your system to create. Every behaviour is meeting a need and every strategy has a positive intention.

What looks like a health problem, may not have anything to do with health at all.

The health pattern

Health is definitely one of the five key areas that is most affected by insecurity. Typically, this is how it shows up:

- Carrying extra weight
- Obsessed with staying skinny
- Frequently sick or have patterns of sickness
- Weird health issues that Doctors can't diagnose
- Lack of energy
- Poor sleep
- Skin issues
- Autoimmune diseases
- You don't feel healthy.

What happens when you try to solve it on this level?

The patterning in the area of health underneath all this, is that you have to fight against yourself to become healthy.

The major thinking problem here is that there is some fat, lazy, recalcitrant part of you that has no interest in succeeding or being healthy. In order to win in life, you must conquer, subdue or even kill this part of you.

This leads to a focus on self-discipline to solve your problems. Convincing yourself that you really just need to be more disciplined, try harder and be better. The only reason that your last efforts didn't succeed can only have been because you just didn't try hard enough! You NEED to be more disciplined!

This thinking leads to the following ineffective behaviour:

- Just trying harder
- Telling yourself to be better
- Beating yourself through self-judgment
- Negative self-talk
- Forcing yourself
- Tricking yourself
- Making deals with yourself
- Fighting against yourself
- Not being able to rest
- Always looking for someone to hold you accountable
- Never feeling you've done enough

The reality is, just because you see pain show up in your health, doesn't mean that you have a health problem.

Do you want to be well?

There is this cool story in the bible about this magic kind of pool that sick people used to camp around in the hope of being healed.[1] The story goes that once a year an angel would appear and stir the water and the first person to dip a toe in would be totally healed.

There is this paralysed guy who has been camped near the pool for 30 years waiting to be healed. One day Jesus walks by and asks him if he'd like to be well. Seems like a strange question. I mean of course he does, right? He's totally committed to being rid of this condition that has afflicted him for most of his life.

The full implications of this question are life changing. If you want to be well then pick up your mat and walk out of here. If you want to be well, then you can't be defined as the sick guy who has no responsibility and has everyone else care for him. You will have to step up and function in the real world, fend for yourself and take full responsibility for your own life. If that's what you want, then you can have it now, magic pool or not.

I'm not saying that sickness isn't real. It's just that sometimes we can be hanging onto it more than it is hanging on to us. It is amazing what we can let go of when we are ready to be free.

---

1   This story is found in John 5:1-15

The point is, this is NOT the battle. Your health is NOT the problem. Trying to fix your health without dealing with your own underlying insecurity can NEVER lead to lasting change. Remember, people work perfectly. Of course you are unhealthy. But your body craves health and is entirely capable of getting you there as you give yourself full permission to flourish.

Accept that being unhealthy is working for you. Sickness gives you rest. Extra weight allows you to hide. Being less than your physical best dials down people's expectations of you in every other area as well.

Sure, you still fail and get judged but it is the sick, tired, fat version of you getting judged, not the real you. If you were to show up at your absolute best and then fail, or be judged and rejected, that would be the ultimate failure!

Rather than fighting yourself to try and make the change, realise that until it is safe for you to show up in the world at your best, then you will continue to be unhealthy as a way of staying safe from what you are afraid of.

Relationship Pain

Jenny's problem – An emotional affair

Jenny came to me in a place of great emotional pain. She explained that her husband had recently had an emotional affair with another woman and that working through this experience was causing her significant distress. Although he sincerely apologised, it had created extreme pain for Jenny and every day since, something would trigger the fresh memory of this experience and she would spiral into a very dark place again. As a result, she feared that she could no longer trust her husband and that their marriage may be over.

As we explored the issue more deeply, it became apparent that there were some gaps in her thinking about the exact problem she was trying to solve.

In order to understand what was really going on for Jenny, I enquired about the kind of pain she was experiencing. Here's how the conversation went:

Tell me what kind of pain are you in here Jenny?

What do you mean? I don't know, I'm just in a lot of pain because my husband had an emotional affair.

Sure. It sounds like you are being very precise here – pain because of an affair, but you haven't actually answered my question. What kind of pain is it? What specifically is painful about your experience here?

It's the pain of being betrayed. Anyone would feel the same if they were betrayed like this.

Let's not worry too much about anyone else, or about being betrayed. What is it about being betrayed that is painful to you?

Well, it's so painful to think about the fact that he has chosen someone else over me. Surely it is totally natural to feel great pain here?!

What's natural is not relevant. What is painful about your husband choosing someone else? What kind of pain is this?

Hmmm...It is the pain of realising that I wasn't good enough or attractive enough to satisfy him. That I wasn't...enough.

So this pain you're experiencing is about your own opinion of yourself?

Oh...you're right.

So, this is not actually a relationship problem, an affair problem, or even a betrayal problem. If it was any of those, Jenny is in real trouble because stating the problem this way gives her no way of fixing things. This is why she already feels hopeless about the situation.

This is an insecurity problem.

Uncovering Jenny's core beliefs about herself revealed these things:

- As a child, her dad had been distant and non-affectionate. On some level she internalised this and made it a reflection of her own value and worth as his daughter.
- From her very first romantic relationship as a teenager, she had looked for someone to give her the love her dad had been incapable of. She craved the safety and certainty it would provide.
- She had put her husband on a pedestal where she believed he could do no wrong. She made it his responsibility to keep her safe by always showing her love. He normally did this very well, but any mistake or incongruent behaviour on his behalf totally rocked her sense of certainty.

The only hope for the relationship moving forward was to solve the real problem first. This was actually a problem about Jenny's opinion and belief about herself which caused her to outsource her need for safety, certainty and love.

Mark's story – Divorce

At 42, Mark had come to me ready to fix his relationship problems. Recently divorced, lonely and isolated he has had a history of pain and suffering in almost all of his adult relationships. The people he most desired to be close to, he held at arm's length, and those who he let in ended up leaving or rejecting him.

His best guess about what created the misery is that he feels deeply afraid of being rejected. This has always been his experience of life. It has led to massive anxiety and resulted in a bunch of dysfunctional patterns. His parents were divorced when he was young, so he's seen rejection first-hand and anticipates it around every corner.

When we turned the lights on and had a clear look beneath the hood, here's what we discovered:

• This rejection fear started at age four when his parents were divorced. The meaning he placed on this event was that it was all his fault. If he'd have cleaned his room more, wasn't so annoying, didn't complain so much, or actually helped his parents when they asked, they would never have got divorced.

25

- He decided he'd made life hard for them. He pushed them apart. He caused their divorce. The opinion he formed about himself was then: "I'm dangerous and ruin peoples lives because of who I am."
- As a result, he formed an opinion about himself that he was a bad person who would always inevitably hurt those he loved if they came too close.
- He'd married his wife only because he identified her as someone incapable of leaving him.
- In the meantime, he was having an affair with someone who was unavailable to have a long-term relationship with him.
- His wife did indeed end the relationship when she realised what he'd done. This proved to him ultimately everyone would reject him.

Clearly, Mark does not have a relationship problem and nor is it a rejection problem. This has always been about his rejection of himself at four.

In order to fix what's happening in his life now, the real problem to solve is the opinion formed by that four-year-old boy.

Rachel's story — Rejection

At 30, Rachel's world had just disintegrated in front of her. Only a few months ago, she appeared to have it all. She was happily married and expecting their first child. She had a good job and was fit and healthy. And then her husband up and left. It was then she realised her success and happiness was an illusion.

When we had a look under the hood we discovered:

- A pattern of placing all her happiness on what others said about her.
- Losing weight to gain acceptance — If I'm beautiful I will be loved by men.
- A deep fear of being rejected.

As we explored the defining moments in her life, she vividly remembered the impact a particular artwork in the family room had on her at three years of age. In the picture there were three people. A loving couple and a girl off to the side looking on jealously. Interestingly, she always identified with the jealous girl. Unconsciously she decided that is the character she would be as well. She believed it was more likely she'd get love through pity of having been rejected than by being accepted.

This story then became the script she lived out of and was therefore a self-fulfilling prophecy.

Of course her husband rejected her! In fact, part of her unconsciously chose him because that's what she knew he would do. That is the path she chose! It turns out there is nothing strange, coincidental or unfair about her relationship history at all.

Clearly Rachel does not have a relationship or rejection problem. It goes far deeper than that into her own relationship with herself.

The relationship pattern

Your key relationships are the second area deeply impacted by personal insecurity. Here is how it typically shows up:

- You settle for relationships that aren't great
- You tolerate other people's bad behaviour
- You get treated poorly no matter how much you try to be assertive
- You end up going last all the time. Everyone else's needs and desires seem to be more important than yours.
- Painful issues are never fully resolved
- You show up needy and desperate
- You feel like a good person by keeping others happy.
- You avoid conflict and doubt yourself
- You always end up sacrificing what you really want for the sake of staying in these relationships

Trying to solve the problem on this level

When we explore the patterning in the area of relationships, there are a few underlying strategies regarding your own sense of value and worth that are always causing the surface level dysfunction.

First of all, you become needy. In order to feel valuable, you need others to validate and accept you. This behaviour leads you to conform to others wishes so that you fit in. It also means you obsess about what others think about you.

Secondly, you become a people pleaser. In order to be a good person, you need to put other's needs before your own. To go first or be assertive may make sense rationally, but it leaves you feeling guilty and selfish which means you end up giving back your power and going last again.

Behaviour mistakes.

This thinking means you try to do well at relationships by:

- Avoiding conflict
- Being a people pleaser
- Becoming the martyr
- Not listening to your own thoughts and feelings
- Doing what others expect and want in order to make them happy
- Accommodating others poor behaviour at your own expense
- Being the 'bigger person'
- Sweeping painful issues under the carpet
- Internalising painful issues
- Manipulating others by playing games and emotional blackmail
- Hoping others will do the right thing by you
- Putting yourself last.

So many people are experiencing significant pain in their closest relationships. While it seems the suffering happens at the hands of their kids, spouse, friends, or boss; this is never the true cause of the pain.

It is probably not a relationship problem

It appears that the relationship issues we face are created outside of us. That is, by hurtful things others say and do. If the perceived problem is with others, then naturally the solution seems to be with them too.

People have let you down. You need people to make it up to you. People have said bad things about you. You need people to say good things to fix the damage. People have diminished or disempowered you. You long for others to see, respect and empower you. The bottom line is you need...

You don't have what it takes to fix this yourself. You look for strong, kind, loving people to make you feel better. They never actually do make you feel better though, because that's not the level this problem really exists on.

Loving relationships

The essence of relating well to another human being comes out of the overflow of our ability to relate to ourselves.

Many years ago, I was school chaplain at my local high school, and I can still clearly remember watching an adult try to encourage one of the students. I was in the middle of talking with someone else but was entirely distracted, watching and listening to the conversation happening nearby.

The teenager had done some small thing well, yet the adult

was praising them as though they'd won an Olympic medal. To say the encouragement was disproportionate to the achievement was a gross understatement.

I enquired about what was happening for the adult in the situation later that morning. Our conversation went along these lines:

I couldn't help but overhear you praising that young lady this morning. I was curious by how passionately you were encouraging her for what sounded like a small win in her life.

Yes, I have the gift of encouragement. I just love to make others feel great by noticing what they do well and fully acknowledging them for it.

Interesting. There was something weird about it though.

What do you mean?

A little over the top, don't you think?

No...I always give as much encouragement as possible no matter how big or small the achievement.

Oh...so there is no light or shade? It's always just full noise? Tell me, how do you feel when others encourage you?

Yuck...I get very awkward. I don't like it at all. I never know what to do with it.

Oh...and how do you go encouraging yourself?

What do you mean? I'm my own worst critic.

So then you don't actually know what true encouragement feels like, and therefore are left to guess how to measure it out to others? Maybe you don't have the gift of encouragement at all. You just want others to think well of you by being so positive?

Obviously, it is impossible to know how to give and receive encouragement to others until you've accurately understood how to encourage yourself.

Love is exactly the same.

Our ability to genuinely give and receive love is made possible by our capacity to deeply give and receive love to ourselves first.

Just because you feel relationship pain, does not mean this is the battle. Your relationships are not the problem. Trying to fix your relationships without dealing with your own underlying insecurity can never lead to lasting change. When you realise that you are in fact 100% responsible for training others how to treat you by what you allow and deny, it helps to show that you've created this mess and it's working for you.

Obviously, the key is to first realise that it is your relationship with yourself that requires the most urgent attention. The ability to give and receive love from another person flows directly out of your ability to deeply love and accept yourself first.

Unhappy Money

Christine's story — Self sabotage

Christine indicated that the main challenge she was facing was to do with her finances. She felt as though she'd worked hard her entire life to get ahead but had very little to show for her efforts.

The central narrative of her life revolved around a very strong Christian faith. This compelled her to be very generous with her time and money to those less fortunate. Her faith also gave her confidence that God would take care of all her needs if she stayed committed to serving the Lord wholeheartedly.

As she explained her situation more fully, there were numerous stories of poor financial management, being taken advantage of by those who appeared to be helping her get ahead, and those whom she was trying to help get ahead. Every investment opportunity she had pursued had ended in a net loss. Additionally, every attempt to improve the value of her assets had ended badly.

Although Christine was in financial difficulty as a result of all these experiences, she was still ever the optimist that God would come through for her.

This blind faith deeply enmeshed with her identity created some significant challenges in our early coaching conversations. However, her willingness to explore the subject more deeply won out, and she made some fascinating discoveries about what was happening beneath the surface.

A few key patterns emerged:

- What looked like generosity was actually her being stolen from. Because she was incapable of saying no without feeling guilty, people would constantly take all her available resources whether she wanted them to or not.
- In order to sleep at night, she could never win if it meant someone else had to lose. In fact, she felt better about herself, if by losing, she had allowed someone else to win.
- No matter how much effort she put into increasing her financial position, her money situation never improved.
- She constantly asked multiple people for their opinion regarding her financial decisions. The information overload then allowed her to action none of the advice.
- As strange as it seemed, the idea of being wealthy was actually scary. As such it became apparent that she unconsciously resisted getting more money.
- Her deepest fears about herself was that she would

    appear greedy or selfish. She could not bear to imagine that someone thought badly of her.

- In fact, her lifelong strategy for feeling like a good person focussed heavily on pleasing others. She had always positioned herself last to make sure others got what they needed.

Clearly Christine does not have a money problem!

The real problem that she was facing was that earning more money would jeopardise her people pleasing strategy. Worse still, if she was no longer able to sacrifice everything for other people's happiness, then she would have no way of telling herself she was a good person.

The deepest issue with Christine was her inability to own her value and worth.

Geraldine's problem – Entrepreneurial fear

Geraldine came to me in a place of pain about her money situation. She was an intelligent, passionate, creative woman with a strong desire to run her own coaching business. She told me the main problem in her life, and where she was stuck, was that the thought of going into debt in the pursuit of this dream was causing massive stress and anxiety.

As a result of this anxiety she constantly felt it would be impossible to let go of the security of a regular wage. She would turn up to her job every day hating the experience, dreaming of leaving and doing her own thing, but feeling as though there was no other option because she just could not go into debt.

In Geraldine's mind she was convinced this was just about needing more financial security. She explained at length that the issue was that she had never liked debt. She told me that financial security was super important and that when she could see enough money in the bank to cover all expenses, then she felt like her life was on track and that she was doing really well.

On the other hand, the moment her bank balance was low, she instantly felt that her whole life was out of control and that nothing was going well.

Her best guess about how to fix the money problem therefore was to be more risk averse. If she could just keep saving as much money as possible, it would create a safe buffer for her to pursue her big dreams without risking her financial security.

The issue with this strategy, as you may have guessed, is that she can never tell how much savings is enough and therefore has no idea how long it will take to guarantee her financial security for the future. This left her feeling like her life was on hold until she had more money.

As a result, she was incredibly torn about what to do. Intuitively she felt that the time was right for her to start her own thing now, yet her bank balance told her otherwise.

So, it looks like a debt problem, a financial security problem, and a safety problem, but this is a long way from the truth. By now I imagine you're getting the point here; there must be a deeper problem.

As I explored this subject with Geraldine, some interesting discoveries emerged.

- After a few experiences of getting into trouble as a child for doing the wrong thing, the prevailing message she received from her mother was that she was not trustworthy.
- This resulted in her having to abide by strict rules and always explain who she was with and what they were doing
- Although her parents were very wealthy, she was only given a small weekly allowance and had to give an account of every dollar spent.
- While Geraldine greatly resented this control and complained of how unfair it was, she personalised her mother's treatment of her and as such unconsciously decided it must be true – She was in fact untrustworthy. There was something wrong with her.

Therefore, the real issue became apparent. The core problem is actually Geraldine's belief that she's not capable of earning enough money to get out of any debt accrued while starting her own business.

That is not a debt problem, or even a money problem. The

problem is clearly in her own opinion of her ability and value. If she was to know her value and worth without a shadow of a doubt and have 100% certainty in her capacity to bring that value to the marketplace, in a way that was incredibly valuable for others, then going into debt becomes entirely irrelevant.

My money story

My first real financial pain came a few years into my entrepreneurial journey. After moving my family to Germany for nine months on a business experiment, funds were running low halfway through the trip. I felt as though I was 100% committed to financial abundance yet was never certain about where my next dollar was coming from.

When I finally got to the core of my money problem, I discovered to my horror that I had in fact been sabotaging my own success. I discovered that deep in my being was embedded a rule that it is impossible to be rich AND godly. Therefore, similar to Christine's story, believed that money would corrupt me and so unconsciously resisted getting more of it.

The real problem had nothing to do with money at all. It was an issue of my own rules about how to be a good person.

After this awareness, I examined the origin of this rule in my life and coached myself through the process of updating it to one that suited my current endeavours.

I decided that these two statements would serve me well:

Insecurity corrupts people not money. Money only magnifies what is inside your heart.

Even if no one else has been rich and godly at the same time, I'm happy to be the first.

Now of course there are plenty of people who've managed to do this, but this statement eradicated my need to find proof that it is possible.

Every day I used these two statements as mantras. While I lived in Germany I would walk in the forest and say these things out loud and on purpose so the trees and squirrels could hear me! I then continued to refine and improve my business plan so that I had clear and compelling offerings to the market. I confidently spoke my message and gave people an opportunity to buy into what I was offering.

In the following two months I almost earned my entire taxable income for the previous year! The fruit of the process finally started to manifest!

The money pattern

Your finances are definitely one of the 5 key areas that is most affected by insecurity.

Typically, this is how it shows up:

- Your financial goals are floundering,
- Struggling to get ahead,
- Not where you thought you'd be by now,
- Lack of confidence affecting your money-making ability,
- Not sure which plan to follow,
- History of poor choices eroding your hope for the future,
- Constant fear of losing the little you've got,
- Poverty/lack mentality,
- Defer to others wisdom,
- Lack of confidence,
- Part of you believes it is dangerous to be wealthy.

Solving it on this level

When people try to solve the problem on this level, the typical ineffective behaviour management strategies are:

- Just sleep less and work harder — the harder you work, the richer you'll become,
- Hope that someone or something else improves your financial situation for you,
- Fantasize about winning lotto / you buy tickets,
- The inner critic must be silenced and suppressed,
- Self-doubt leading to procrastination,
- Subconscious self-sabotage
- Comparing you to others,
- Taking on too much debt to keep up with the Jones',
- Staying in your dead-end job,
- Serving someone else's vision,
- Trusting the system,

- Never examining your story,
- Not being clear about what you really want,
- Settling and surviving,
- False hope,
- Suppress the fear and pretend it is not there. Remain in the dark about the whole money thing,
- Defer to the financial wisdom of others.

It's probably not a money problem.

The point is, just because you feel pain on the level of your finances doesn't mean that's where the real problem lies. All the financial strategies in the world don't have the power to truly fix the issue if you don't have internal permission to be wealthy.

Some people are insecure about HAVING more money. They are driven to prove they are a good person by not being rich. The fear is money will corrupt them. More money will make them greedy, selfish and arrogant. Therefore, money is dangerous and having money will expose them as a bad person.

Other people are insecure about NOT HAVING more money. They are driven to prove their value and worth by showing the world how awesome they are by how rich they can be. Therefore, money is safe. Having no money makes you worthless.

Neither of these problems are actually about money. It is simply where the problem is showing up.

Your money story

Ken Honda, in his fantastic book *Happy Money*[2] introduces the idea that money is far from a concrete reality. Even though you can see, touch and exchange the physical form of money, it is far less real than most people imagine.

Imagine walking along the beach and seeing $20 washed up on the sand in front of you. Honda says there are all kinds of possibilities about what happens next, all depending on your relationship with money. Do you pick it up or leave it there? If you pick it up, do you keep it or try to give it away. If you give it away, who to? Your kids, or a poor person? Do you try and find the owner? Do you give it to a lifeguard or police officer? If you keep it, do you feel guilty? Do you spend it or save it?

You get the point. There are many different endings to the story based on what happens internally when you come into contact with that $20. In fact, the moment you do come into contact with the money, it becomes an extension of you. It is instantly transformed to become a representation of what is in your head and heart. It magically becomes different for each hand it touches.

When you see the truth of this idea it is completely life changing. It means you currently have a relationship with money. That

---

2   Ken Honda, *Happy money,*

relationship has been developed and cultivated over time to be as it is right now; yet, because it is a relationship it is alive and entirely changeable.

A person's relationship with money is one of the clearest windows into the heart of their relationship with themselves. Because we use money to ascribe value to things, what we believe about money and our patterns of behaviour around money, help us to see the value we place on ourselves.

Because it is not common to observe deeper patterns or dig into the subconscious patterning that so clearly drives our life, most people have no idea that they even have a relationship with money let alone that that relationship is connected to all other relationships.

If you haven't sorted through your money story, then often the subconscious script you are living out of is actually locking you out of financial abundance because in your story your deepest beliefs are that:

- Money will corrupt you,
- Money is dangerous,
- Rich people are bad people,
- There is not enough to go around,
- You don't deserve to get what you want,
- It is selfish and greedy to want more than you have,
- The more you chase it, the less you get,

Behaviour never lies. It always proves what we really believe. So, to gain some awareness about your beliefs around money, simply observe your patterns of behaviour when it comes to keeping and losing the coin.

Some useful questions to ponder:

- What did your parents teach you about money?
- What did they model about money?
- Was money hard or easy growing up?
- Were rich people good or bad?
- What pain did you experience around money?
- What internal vows did you make to yourself about money?

Therefore, your money is not where the main problem is. Trying to 'fix' your finances without dealing with your own underlying beliefs about yourself and money can NEVER lead to lasting change.

Your current financial position is directly affected by your money story, which was often created when you were very young, without you really being aware. Your relationship with money is actually one of the clearest indications of your relationship with yourself, therefore, money issues are entirely connected to the insecurity problem.

Money is the reward you get for accurately understanding your value to the world.

Obviously, we all have great value. We also deserve to have that value reflected back to us in every way possible. But that's never going to be enough. The onus is on each of us to truly dive into our own essence and accurately know and understand our unique value rather than to wait for the world to give us what we deserve.

I'm convinced that money is one of the natural rewards for doing this work. It proves we have done it well. I think it is impossible to accurately understand your value and also be poor. Most people avoid accurately understanding their value for fear of getting it wrong and being judged or ridiculed.

Work is sucking the life out of you

Scott's story — The golden handcuffs

Scott decided he was ready for change and the key challenge in his life was what he described as 'the golden handcuffs.'

Scott was in a FIFO (fly in/fly out) mining job job that paid really well, but his desire was to leave and pursue a career in real estate. This was much more aligned with the dream he had for his life and would be a much healthier lifestyle for his family. He hated the work, being away from his family for so long and the toxic culture of the workplace. But, in his mind, the only reason he hasn't left already is simply because the money is so good.

The danger of labels

This is not a money issue, nor is it a work issue.

Language doesn't just describe our reality it shapes it. Having cool labels on our problems only serves to give these experiences a concrete reality and further embed them into our life as immovable objects with a life of their own.

When Scott took a step back, turned all the lights on and observed his life objectively, he began to see these patterns emerge:

- Saying it was all about the money was just a cover up for what he was afraid of.
- Blaming his wife for their financial situation became another useful hideout from the real issue. (His wife had tried starting her own business, which was unsuccessful, and had used up all the surplus funds they'd saved.)
- It allowed him to be the hero/martyr in the story for continuing to be financially responsible.
- 'Golden handcuffs' meant it wasn't something he could control. It's a real thing that lots of people have to battle with.
- If he never quit the job and started his own real estate thing, then he could never fail or be found out as not good enough.

Rahini's story – Value and worth

Rahini had been working as an assistant for many years but wanted to be a manager. She decided to get some further qualifications without telling anyone at work. Shortly after she completed her studies the business sold. The new owners took over and the current manager left. She told them she had the qualifications to step up as manager.

The new owners asked her to suggest what she thought she was worth and set up a meeting two days later. After some research, she suggested a $12 per hour increase and took that to the meeting. They responded by suggesting a $2 per hour increase with a chance to review after an initial trial period. She was so keen for the role and saw no other job offers around, so said yes.

It all started well, but then the work increased, and the pay stayed the same. Her boss became more and more demanding and was increasingly difficult to keep happy. There were so many requirements for her to attend to that she was constantly overwhelmed. Most of them outside the scope of the initial role she'd agreed to which meant she never felt like she had the chance to demonstrate her real value.

Rahini tried to address the issue with the owners, and things would improve briefly, but then go back to the way they were in a very short time. She felt frustrated, underappreciated and demotivated.

Surely this a work problem?

Even though there are laws to protect the rights of employees to prevent this kind of thing from happening, they don't address the real issue here.

Let's explore this problem by being as precise as possible.

Firstly, what appears to be a work problem, is actually a relationship problem. It is one person feeling as though they are being undervalued and treated poorly by another person.

Going one level deeper. What appears to be a relationship problem is actually a neediness problem.

Although it seems Rahini is doing everything she can to address the issue and that it's her boss's fault for treating her badly, the real reason she is stuck in this situation is because she has given all her power away in exchange for what she needs.

Her boss is definitely not the one with the problem here. He is getting everything he wants and Rahini is giving it to him. Sure, he's hurting her, but only because of what she needs from him.

As I explain in my first book, *Elegantly Simple Solutions to Complex People Problems,* the only people who have the power to hurt us are those we need something from.

When I explored this idea with Rahini, this is what was revealed:

- She liked telling friends and family that she was now a manager rather than just an assistant. It gave her a feeling of significance and success. However, she was insecure about her skills, value and experience in this new position.
- As a result, she needed to cling to this role. She saw it as her only opportunity for a role like this in her industry.
- Therefore, to be more assertive with her boss and demand

better treatment, she runs the risk of upsetting her boss and then ultimately losing her job.

- He has what she needs. He then has the power to hurt her by withholding the thing she needs. Because she needs what he has, she then has to tolerate whatever his behaviour is towards her.

This kind of situation happens all the time! There is no point complaining about the boss behaving badly. They own you. It's their world, their business, their money. They risked it all to start their own thing and you are benefiting from their entrepreneurial courage. They actually can do whatever they want while ever you need what they are giving you.

You can't fix this problem by trying to deal with it as a work issue, or even a relationship issue. The neediness must be addressed first.

So, the key coaching question therefore is – do you really *need* this job?

Of course, that then reveals some deeper issues:

- If I'm not a manager, then who am I?
- Maybe I'm not as good a manager as I thought I was.
- Maybe I'm not worth as much money as I thought I was.
- If I lose my job, what if I can't find other work. I'm not sure what else I could do?
- What will I tell people if I'm unemployed?

The work pattern

Underneath all this:

- Your job is killing you
- You're bored and unstimulated
- You live for the weekend
- You are constantly frustrated by all the waste, inefficiencies and poor practice within the workplace.
- You could do your job with your eyes closed.
- You're serving someone else's vision and solving someone else's problems.
- Your boss is an idiot

The key question has to be, so why are you still there?

It is not because of the money, not because of the friends you've made, and not because you're good at what you do. None of these reasons are enough to keep you rocking up to a job that is literally sucking the life out of you.

The ONLY reason we tolerate or complain about the things that are less than ideal in our life, yet do not change them, is that they MUST be working for us. To remain in the situation has to be protecting you from what you are most afraid of. That is, being found out as inadequate or somehow not good enough. As much as you hate working for the man, the man is keeping you safe.

This is not a work problem.

Work pain is such a common theme for people, especially those who are into their 30's and 40's. Again, the default is to believe the problem is entirely work related because that's where you see the pain show up. But if you treat the pain by simply moving jobs, getting a raise or negotiating better conditions with your boss, the issue inevitably resurfaces shortly thereafter.

The point is, the problem is NOT with your job. It is another manifestation of the deepest doubts, fears and insecurities lurking in the dark. The cool thing, however, is eventually your job is supposed to be a world of pain for you! And that pain is trying to get your attention about the deeper reality you need to face up to.

Did you know that after a while your job is supposed to suck?

If you were to stop and ask the first 10 people you came across today, to tell you about their job, I'll guarantee you'll hear some painful stories. Most people do not love their work. More than that, most people experience high levels of stress, frustration and pain around their employment situation.

The interesting news is that after a while your job is supposed to suck. Pain is guaranteed. In fact, it is actually normal, healthy and to be entirely expected that you will grow to hate your day job.

The gift of pain

Pain is actually a gift designed to protect you from doing major damage to yourself. It is all about keeping you safe, happy and healthy. Pain is your most honest voice. It is there to tell you to make changes.

Sooner or later, working for the man is going to create major pain in your life. There is nothing surer. Now, rather than that being a huge problem, it's actually a wonderful thing. The pain is there to let you know that it is time to keep growing. To find your voice, and your sweet spot, and step beyond the comfort of the system into the realm of the entrepreneur.

The pain of the job you now hate is telling you to stick it to the man and take control of your life. To create a lifestyle around doing work that you enjoy and are good at and something that gives you the ability to leave your unique mark on the world.

If you ignore the pain and tell yourself to suck it up because this is as good as it gets, no one could blame you. Chasing your own dreams is really hard. Serving someone else's dream means you never really have to stick your neck out and see what you are capable of. You can't fail if you never fully try. Yet choosing to suppress the pain inevitably starts to cause atrophy of mind, heart and soul. You end up as a mindless consumer, soothing the pain with various ugly self-medication strategies.

(N.B. If you are 17 and not enjoying your job at KFC, don't stick it to the man just yet. There are still plenty of important life lessons about being a responsible adult working as a good employee for you to learn before you are ready to move on.)

Business problems

If you've already stuck it to the man and pursued your entrepreneurial vision, here's how work problems show up differently.

My research shows that unresolved insecurity shows up as one or more of these 5 things:

- Lack of assertiveness/certainty — Your ability to say yes and no at the appropriate time is compromised. You show up on the back foot and there is no certainty in the way you lead yourself and others. You have a weak presence that repels your ideal clients. This leads to self-sabotage, poor leadership and missed opportunities.
- Undervaluing your products and services — You settle for less than you are worth. You show up needy and desperate. You end up selling to those who can't afford you, which are not your ideal clients. This leads to you attracting the wrong clients, undervaluing your time and skills and therefore, struggling to sell.
- Unrealised potential — You know that you have a mountain of value, but you just can't back yourself enough to communicate that to the market. You constantly watch your competitors with fewer skills, experience and quality, do better than you. This leads to a sense of injustice and jealousy as you watch yourself falling behind your competitors.
- Motivation has gone missing — Procrastination, exhaustion, sickness, self-sabotage. It's almost like part of you is working against your own success. The important stuff just never gets done. This leads to avoidance, procrastination,

feeling tired/sick/lazy and fighting against yourself to do better.

- Speed drop — Everything has slowed down. Meetings, decisions, improvements, problem solving and asset development all takes ages! It's like you're driving the car with the handbrake on. This leads to constant bottlenecks, inefficiencies, mistakes and poor execution.

Clearly this is not a work problem or a business problem, but an insecurity problem.

It is likely that your business and marketing plans are fine. It's your ability to be the kind of person that can execute them effectively. That is the real issue. Success is a science. The question is, are you able to be the scientist capable of success?

No Purpose

Trudy's story – Making better choices

Trudy called me in tears. We'd done a coaching intensive a few months prior, which had greatly impacted her sense of clarity and confidence, yet she had now found herself stuck again and it was causing some intense pain.

She was frustrated, disappointed and upset. The things she'd committed to in our last session had not been done and she explained that she was still constantly making poor life choices that were not making her happy. She was deeply annoyed that she continued to procrastinate about the actions she knew would move her closer to her dreams and was at a loss as to understand why this was happening.

When I asked her to be as specific as possible about the real problem she was facing, her best answer was that she needed to make better choices. "I know I can be better," she said. "I've just got to discipline myself to face my fears and get it done! My problem is that I'm weak. I just need to be stronger."

OK Trudy...are you sure that's the problem? If that really is the problem, we have a bigger problem. You've tried being better, bigger, stronger before and it hasn't worked. You're still stuck.

I told her that from my side of the table things looked very different and as such I wasn't convinced her diagnosis was accurate. I reminded her not to confuse me for someone who cared about her current situation.

I don't need anything from you. I'm not impacted by your pain in any way. I don't need it to be anything other than it is which means I am free to see it for what it really is. There is zero judgment here Trudy. You know that is true. I'm not another person who wants you to do something you don't want to do. As your life coach, my only agenda here is to serve you to get more of what you want.

I then invited her to slide around to my side of the table to see how different things looked from here.

So, what's really happening here Trudy? When you remove the frustration, disappointment and judgment can you see what the real problem is?

I still don't have permission to succeed. There is still more fear associated with success than failure. My unconscious is lovingly keeping me from being found out as inadequate by leaving the handbrake on so I stay exactly where I am.

Uh huh. That seems like a kind thing of your unconscious to do. That's a very different problem than when we started this conversation. And what conditions would need to be satisfied before you did have permission to move forward into the things you truly desire?

I'd have to fully own my value and worth as a person and believe I am enough with nothing to prove or defend, rather than continuing to need my friends and family to approve of me. I'd have to solve the insecurity problem. Then I'd be free.

The happiness pattern

- Suppressed hopes and dreams,
- Residual disappointment,
- Lowered expectations — The best way to not get hurt is to have no expectations.

Leads to the following behaviour:

- Regressing back to the last happy place,
- Shutting down uncertainty, questions, doubt.
- Feeling unhappy, stuck, frustrated, unfulfilled,
- Making no progress,
- Feeling like life has no meaning.

At every new level of growth, there is always a season of chaos, and uncertainty as our old strategies are proving ineffective and we have yet to build new systems of living.

On the Tim Ferris podcast, Derek Sivers says that the longer you can sit in uncertainty without rushing to fill it, the more profound the new thing will be when you finally emerge.[3]

It's probably not a purpose problem

To solve the purpose problem, you need to solve the insecurity problem first. "The two most important days of your life are the day you are born and the day you find out why" — Mark Twain.

Finding your life's purpose is perhaps the most meaningful journey you will ever undertake. To solve the purpose problem, start with what the answer is not. Your purpose is NOT to try to inspire others.

While many social media influencers orient their whole message around drawing attention to their achievements, and triumphs over adversity with the stated intention of inspiring others to do the same, no one is actually inspired to anything great by someone telling them to be great.

The people who inspire me most have not once told me that's what they were trying to do. Your purpose is not to prove other people wrong. People do all kinds of remarkable things purely

---

3   Episode 135 of the Tim Ferris Show. https://tim.blog/2015/12/14/derek-siv-ers-on-developing-confidence-finding-happiness-and-saying-no-to-millions/

motived by the haters, naysayers and doubters who've all told them they can't or won't. Yet when the seemingly impossible achievement is reached, they are often no more fulfilled than when they began. Surely true purpose has to be bigger and more beautiful than that.

It is the universal fear of not being good enough that drives people to fill their cup externally. They seek validation from the world based on the size and strength of what they can do. They use what looks like purpose to prove their worth and value. To prove they can contribute, to prove they can inspire others, to prove they can change the world. It *cannot* be your purpose to prove that you matter.

Your work is to discover your inherent worth separate from what you do or have or what anyone else thinks of you – then you are free to really connect with purpose. You now go into the world with your cup full. You now have something to give. You are now free to contribute out of the essence of who you are and connect with a purpose that is bigger than you and not about you.

The people who make the most significant contributions to the world do so from a place of wholeness. If you want to connect with the purpose for your life, you'll need to solve the insecurity problem first.

So why haven't you; a creative, intelligent good person, solved these problems already?

The Insecurity Problem

The wrong problem

People typically try and solve their problems on the same level that the pain shows up. Because they experience pain with their health, they imagine it is a health problem. When they feel pain in their finances, it is assumed to be a money problem. Or, when the pain manifests in their relationships with others, it is natural to believe it is a relationship problem.

The issue here is that because this surface level pain is merely the symptom of deeper dysfunction, all time, money and effort spent solving the problem on this level is wasted.

Often people imagine their behaviour is somehow disconnected from any other area of their life. It somehow exists on its own, in a vacuum. This belief is bolstered by the cultural proclivity for behaviour management strategies as the best way to do personal change.

However, any level of clear thinking about this idea shows how deeply flawed it is. Behaviour is simply the by-product of belief. Behaviour never lies. It is an accurate reflection of our map of the world and always proves what we believe to be true. Behaviour is simply the product at the end of the assembly line. Your behaviour is not weird, mysterious, or anomalous. To view your life in this way is such a lazy observation.

While behaviour management is typically the go-to strategy for self-development, it can never create lasting change. What's more, to fight against your own behaviour using self discipline and willpower is not only counter productive, it is incredibly unkind.

To genuinely change any behaviour long term, first requires you to understand the belief that is producing it. Always start with behaviour because that is what you can see, but then you must dive into what you can't see to sort out what is actually going on.

Therefore, the transformation process is always a journey into the unseen world. It requires curiosity, inquiry and deeper forms of awareness.

Back to our two problem-solving questions:

1. What problem are you most trying to solve right now?
2. Are you sure that is actually the problem?

The key here is to see that the deepest fear is always your own opinion of yourself. That is why this process is so exciting. Opinions can be changed. Especially when they're your own.

The thing about fear is that it predominately sits on a level of abstraction that goes unobserved. It is very rare for people to be clear about what they are actually afraid of. If they were aware of the exact nature of their fear, they would not be nearly as afraid. Fear is irrational. We don't fear the thing — we fear the thought of the thing, the imagination of the thing, the story about the thing, the symptoms of the thing, and the exaggeration of the thing.

The child with nightmares is not afraid of the monster under the bed; they are terrified of the thought of the monster. They have never actually turned the lights on and had a look under the bed in case their imagination is true.

You are not afraid of not being enough; you are afraid of the imagination of this idea and you've never actually had a look under the bed to see if it is true.

Here's how this works though. Fear unexamined grows. Fear examined is diminished. Fear unexamined is irrational. Fear examined is never as bad as the thought of the fear. Fear unexamined becomes a monster that will consume you. Fear examined is a couple of mice playing silly buggers with shadows and echoes. When fully examined, the deepest level of the problem is simply your own opinion of yourself.

This is the problem to be solved. This is the insecurity problem.

Insecurity is something we all battle on some level. It is the *real* problem we face that is causing all the things we think are our problems in life. Underneath almost every relational, emotional, social, financial and even physical issue is some kind of limiting belief about our own value and worth.

Insecurities are like the handbrake that severely limits your ability to flourish in life. Therefore, to leave insecurity festering beneath the surface becomes incredibly costly for every area of life! It is out of our insecurities that we end up consistently hurting ourselves and those around us. It causes us to act out of our ego in an attempt to defend and prove ourselves to the world. It is an epidemic of insecurity that is responsible for much of the madness in the world today. Left untreated it will destroy you.

Most people are too afraid of delving into the fear of their own inadequacy and so try and suppress their insecurity in the hope it can be controlled or managed. Yet, inevitably our insecurities cannot be contained, they must be faced. The beautiful thing is that the moment you find the courage to do so, you discover they are works of fiction. You have always been enough and always will be. It is possible to live your life without insecurity. Let me show you how.

Unaddressed insecurity will lead to madness

It is common for people to either be insecure about being insecure or be unaware that they are insecure.

In addition to the health, relationship, work, finance and happiness indicators; here are another fifteen clear signs that may indicate if you are acting out of insecurity. And I'll warn you now. This list isn't pretty:

1. Everything feels personal. Every event, conversation and experience is interpreted through the fear of not being enough. You are always edgy about what is going on around you because everything touches you personally.

2. Dominance. You have to have the last word. You feel the need to prove your worth to the world by always being right and in control.

3. Attention seeking. You always need to be the centre of attention and constantly seek approval and validation from your world to make you feel better about yourself.

4. Selfishness. The most insecure people are always the most selfish as well. If you don't get taken care of by others, then you fear you will go without. You have to make sure your needs are always met by those around you.

5. Defensiveness. You feel you have to protect your image, and make sure you are always seen in the best light. You can't afford anyone to see through the game playing and façade you are holding up.

6. Can't say sorry. You never back down and find it very difficult to apologise. You have no reverse gear. Once you are engaged in something, even if you are wrong, you can't

back down and admit your mistake. The underlying logic is: if you've done something wrong or bad, then you must be bad. The only option then is to defend your position instead, no matter what.

7. Jealousy eats at you. You are always comparing yourself with what everyone else is doing, and has, and looking over the fence feeling that others have it better than you.

8. Bullying. You put others down through gossip and slander. By highlighting other's weaknesses, you get to elevate yourself above them.

9. Bitterness. You are fantastic at holding a grudge. A great way of proving you are better than others is by never allowing them to forget their mistakes.

10. Overreacting. Because everything is personal, tiny issues become life and death issues. Things escalate quickly and you get angry and frustrated over trivial things that aren't that big a deal in the scheme of things.

11. Finger pointing. There is a high level of blame and excuse in your life. You constantly externalise your issues so you avoid having to take responsibility. Nothing is your fault or your responsibility. You deeply fear being found out as inadequate or not enough, so you constantly deflect the attention by pointing the finger at others.

12. Frustration. You are often angry and frustrated at others. Frustration with others is actually about your deep frustration with yourself. It's just easier to point out others stupidity than deal with your own flaws and mistakes.

13. Hiding. You are unhealthy and overweight. Carrying extra weight is almost always a hide out. You don't like the way you look which adds to your insecurity, but at least people don't expect you to be awesome, so you can't really disappoint them and you don't have to put yourself out there.

14. Guardedness. You always remain in your strength. Vulnerability is terrifying. You find ways to play the game in a way that means you never lose. You never do things that you are not good at where others may perceive you as weak or inadequate.

15. Point scoring. You always have something to prove. You can never relax or rest. You are constantly promoting yourself and are driven to prove your worth to the world by what you can achieve and accomplish. You sometimes lie or embellish the truth to make yourself look better.

Insecurity left unaddressed can only lead to a form of madness. It will cause you to show up at your worst where it matters most and rob you of experiencing an authentic experience of who you really are.

Take the insecurity test and find out where insecurity is costing you the most:

www.jaeminfrazer.com

Ideal Conditions

The impact of insecurity on performance.

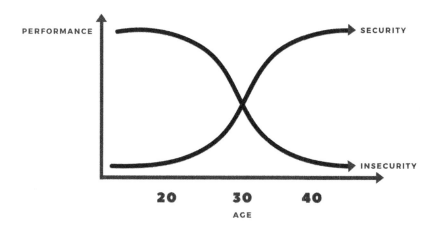

This diagram highlights the impact insecurity has on relation-ship between performance capacity and age.

Insecurity

In the judgment-free space, insecurity is neither good nor bad. If we explore the impact insecurity has on your ability to gener-ate real results, you may be surprised. In fact, insecurity may be the thing driving up performance in your 20's. It is often the most insecure young people who do the most extraordinary things. Being driven to desperately prove your value and worth to the world by what you can achieve is a powerful source of motivation.

This driven-ness makes people unrealistic, unreasonable and irrational, all of which drives up their performance capacity. The word NO does not compute as a reason to stop. In fact, it becomes the trigger to ramp up the intensity of their desire to prove that NO is wrong. The best way to motivate an insecure 20-year-old is to tell them they can't or won't. The word no is like rocket fuel.

At the time of writing this book, the 10-part Netflix documentary on Michael Jordan had just been released. One of the most remarkable things of the Jordan backstory is the exposé into what drove him to perform at such a high level.

Initially, it was the need to be recognised in the same category as Magic Johnston and Larry Bird as one of the all-time greats, but soon it became the drive to be the greatest. Jordan was unquestionably one of the most talented players the world had ever seen, but what unleashed the true superstar in him was the drive to prove he was better than everyone else. The moment someone appeared to cast shade on him or outperform him, it instantly became personal. This lit a fire inside him where failure was removed from the list of possible outcomes. From that moment it was win at all costs. No matter what.

This is the power insecurity has to drive up performance. Such

was Jordan's need to declare his power to the world by dominating others, there was nothing that could get in his way.
By the end of his reign as the best sportsman the world had
ever seen, it could be argued that he was aware of the power
being personally slighted gave him and, therefore, deliberately
attracted and hung onto such events to give him the necessary
performance boost. In fact, he even went as far as fabricating a
story of an opponent sledging him after a game just so he could
use it as fuel to outperform this player in the following match.

While Michael Jordan's example highlights the wonderful performance enhancing drug of insecurity from 20–30 years old, it
also beautifully demonstrates the downturn as the years pass
by.

Being fuelled by insecurity is unsustainable. It creates massive
collateral damage, especially to relationships and health, and
ultimately creates exhaustion and burnout. By the time Jordan
had won his 6th championship, he was mentally and physically
wiped out. Whether he could have gone on to win another title
with the Bulls, had the management not dismantled the team,
is forever debated. But what cannot be disputed is that sooner
or later, some young buck would eventually rise up and take his
crown. It is one thing to dominate all comers at 30, but if you
still need to prove to the world how great you are at 40, you'll
be laughed off the court. Your mouth will be writing cheques
your body cannot cash.

To be still driven to prove your awesomeness to the world at

40 years old is incredibly exhausting. Not only are you running out of steam, but those around you are tired of you as well. It becomes harder and harder to force yourself to perform and the insecure 40-year-old is increasingly lonely and isolated.

From 40-50, insecure people either give up on their own performance goals altogether or transfer their ambition for significance into their kids' performance. If proving their value and worth through their own results can't work anymore, then maybe they will show they matter by having their children achieve great things.

It is important to state that insecurity in a person's 20's may also result in paralysis and inaction. At its best, insecurity will be a powerful motivator for all kinds of wonderful and bold action. At its worst, it will cause a person to run away and hide.

The point is, insecurity is more likely to drive up results than security is at this point in life.

Security

In contrast, the secure 20-year-old will often show up in the world pretty relaxed. If there is nothing to prove or defend, it doesn't really matter what they do. Their confidence may cause them to be more realistic about their lack of skills and knowledge. Then they would be more inclined to settle down, wait their turn, learn their craft and accept their place in the world. Compared with their driven friends, it would often appear that they are significantly under-performing.

In general, this relationship between insecurity and performance starts to change at around 30 years of age. This is often where insecurity starts to cost you more than it is benefiting you. On the other hand, this is also the point where security starts paying off in terms of your capacity to perform at your best. From age 30-40, this trend continues significantly.

Intimate relationships can be built on insecurity successfully in your 20's but put two insecure people together for 10 years and they will have sucked each other dry. If both parties fail to solve their insecurity problem, it spells disaster for the relationship.

Secure people's relationships start to really blossom in their 30's and 40's. They've done the groundwork together, sorted through most of the significant conflict two people face when joining their lives together, and are ready to capitalise on the fruit of their labours.

At the time of writing this book, my wife and I are both 41 years old and have been married since 19. The deep personal development work we have both done overcoming insecurity in the last ten years has strengthened us and brought a richness to our relationship. We are more in love than we've even been and are incredibly excited about our future together.

There is no way we could have done this work in our 20's. We were both finding our way in our careers, grappling with the overwhelming challenges of being new parents, and were desperate to prove that we could be responsible adults.

This is also true in the areas of finance, career, health, and happiness. Being driven to prove something is useful in your 20's but that insecurity will start causing grief into your 30's. As you head towards mid-life however, it is deep personal security in your own value and worth that radically drives up performance in every area of your life instead.

The point is, before you reach 30, insecurity may be working really well for you. In that case, it doesn't make sense to resolve the fear driving you at this point in your life. However, the older you get, less advantages can be found trying to prove yourself. Unresolved insecurity is now inevitably leading you towards madness. That is the only possible outcome.

As you age, insecurity becomes the number one inhibitor of performance in life and business and it is security that opens up new levels of growth and success. Therefore, until you solve the insecurity problem in your life, you'll never achieve your potential.

Solving the insecurity problem for good is entirely dependent on readiness for change.

Readiness for change

Change is hard.

People often overestimate their readiness for change and frequently miscalculate the costs involved. Dealing with unresolved insecurity will more than likely be the hardest personal development work you will ever do.

As a coach, the very first thing I assess is a person's readiness for change. In my experience based on over 10,000 hours of coaching, some clear patterns have emerged that would indicate when a person is truly ready for change and when they are not.

Interestingly, one of the most significant factors around this readiness is often a person's age. In my experience, readiness and the capacity for lasting change peaks at 40 years of age. In my observation, if there was a time in life most conducive to do this deep change work, it is somewhere around 35-45 years old.

Admittedly, there are many variables at play and things that contribute to readiness that I have not explicitly examined, however, in my observation, statistically 68% of the population will be most ready for change within the 35-45 window. 13.5% will be at peak readiness at 30 or at 50 and only 2.35% will be ready at 25 or 55. The great thing about the Bell curve [1]is that it clearly represents the outliers. There will always be people who are way ahead of the curve and are ready for deep change at 20 years old. And, equally there will always be those who are completely ready and willing at 60. Obviously, you can change whenever you want. The point is, that the further outside the 35-45 change window you are, the harder the change process will be.

It is never too late to change your life until it is.

The personal change bell curve.

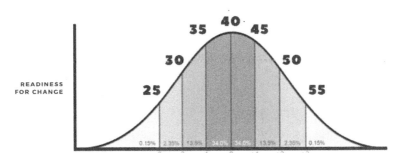

Here's what makes the 35-45 year age group such an effective change window for solving the insecurity problem:

a) The pain levels are just right

As you will see in stage three of overcoming insecurity, pain is essential to all personal change. In general, 20-year olds don't have enough pain, and 60-year olds have too much. At 40 years old, there is certainly a lot of existential pain, yet it is also mixed with a sense of hope for the future. While the pain levels are high, there is also the awareness that it is not too late. Although time is running out, there is still enough time to turn things around. There is a sense of urgency that it's now or never.

In your 20's you assume you'll have all your shit together by 40. Arriving closer and closer to that age, you realise you're a long way from having it all sorted! And that brings about a lot of pain. The sense of pain at mid-life often comes with unavoidable deep questioning of all that you've done with your life. This pain drives up readiness for change because the inescapable truth is that things won't automatically fix themselves unless you do something drastically different.

b) You are ready to be wrong about stuff

You realise you are wrong about a whole bunch of things you've always been closed and sure about. Best-selling author Mark Manson devotes a whole chapter to this idea in his book *The Subtle Art of Not Giving A F*Ck*. He suggests that it's worth remembering that for any change to happen, you must be wrong about something. And until you are able to question yourself to find it, nothing will change.[4] It turns out that being wrong is essential for growth and change.

"A man is usually 35 before he realizes that his 'job life', and his relationships with women, and with other men, are not working."[5]

ROBERT BLY

In your middle years, life has beaten some of the idealism out of you while not turning you bitter and hard hearted yet. The knocks and falls have given you humility and openness to learning. There is often a level of acceptance of the current reality rather than projection and fantasy about how they'd like things to be. 20-year olds often know too much while 60-year olds are too set in their ways.

---

4   "The only way to solve our problems is to first admit that our actions and beliefs up to this point have been wrong and are not working. This openness to being wrong must exist for any real change or growth to take place" *The Subtle Art of not Giving a F*ck.* P.134

5   https://www.latimes.com/archives/la-xpm-1991-03-19-vw-472-story.html

There is a realism that comes with being 40 that opens your heart to new and different ways of thinking that idealism and pessimism locks you out of.

The role of failure plays a key part in the willingness to be wrong. While failure inevitably brings a measure of suffering with it, it also opens us to new possibilities like nothing else. The experience of embarrassment, disappointment and self-berating that come with failure create a desperation to never have this happen again. Admittedly, this can cause a person to retreat from life, but it also provides maximum opportunity for self-reflection and growth. The value of being wrong cannot be understated. We learn more from being wrong and falling on our face then by being right could ever teach us.

c) You are more likely to know what you really want

The instruction to follow your dreams as a teenager leads you down all kinds of strange and weird paths. For example, my high school dreams included being a marine biologist, physio-therapist, landscape architect, and becoming an engineer in the army. In the end, none of these things eventuated as I pursued a career as a church pastor instead! I look back at this list and wonder what I was thinking. I can't imagine what possessed me to imagine I'd enjoy being in the army, yet at 18, that is all I wanted to do. Award winning author Maria Popova says "You discover your dream or sense of purpose in the very act of walking the path"[6]

---

6   Tim Ferris, *Tools of Titans,* Vermilion, London, 2016, *p410*

An increased sense of increased clarity about what you want in life often starts with an aching awareness of what you don't want. This happens mid-life as the pain levels increase as mentioned above. You're ambitious to do something meaningful with your life before it's too late.

Being aware that you are not satisfied with your current position and are still ambitious to live a meaningful existence is an essential aspect of readiness for change. Without change, your life will continue to flounder and stagnate. You must take control of your destiny and do something different.

d) Emotional intelligence and maturity

40 years in your own skin is a long time. It is likely that all this time being you has allowed you to observe what you are really like. There is more awareness about your inherent strengths and weaknesses and the patterns of behaviour that keep showing up despite your best efforts to change or eradicate them. With this emotional intelligence comes the awareness that the major hindrances are all inside you in the form of doubts, fears and limiting beliefs rather than about what anyone else is doing or not doing. You realise that their biggest battle is inside your own heart and mind. It is not the external factors like lack of time, money, skills or support.

At 40 years old, it is more likely that you've made it out of the survival mode that comes with having toddlers in the house. There is also a good chance you've found some kind of financial stability and are settled in a career or business. No longer being in survival mode gives you the chance to focus thought and energy on personal development and deeper life issues.

e) Cultural expectations and allowances

40-year olds are allowed, and almost expected, to make a few big changes. You are half-way through your working life, and now is a good time to pivot into the next season. The term mid-life crisis is used to understand and justify all kinds of dramatic changes made in this season of life. Typically, we afford friends and family much more grace to change everything at 40 than we do at 25.

People are more inclined to make decisions to do things differently on New Year's Eve, or their birthday or anniversary. Turning 30 often triggers feelings of unhappiness and dissatisfaction with life. It is much harder to pretend you are still a child with no care or responsibility. It is time to settle down and start taking life more seriously. If you haven't done these things by now there is pressure to decide on a career path, to settle down with a life partner and consider starting a family.

Obviously, we could make change at any moment in time, but having an external trigger certainly seems to help. Arbitrary milestones provide a reason to give yourself permission to make desired change.

f) Ready to move from level 4 to 5

The Spiral Dynamics model first created by Dr Clare. W Graves and published by Chris Cowan and Don Beck is one of the most useful frameworks for understanding the path and process of growth as a human being.

The 7 levels of consciousness we can grow through are:

1. Survival
2. Tribe
3. Rebellion
4. The system
5. Entrepreneur
6. Contribution
7. Statesmanship

Typically, people move from level 3 to 4 in their early 20's and are ready to move from 4 to 5 in their late 30's or early 40's.

The longer a person remains at level 3 (rebellion), without learning the crucial lessons of this stage and moving on, the more likely they are to become misfits, conspiracy theorists and socially isolated.

The natural growth process is that the teenage rebel settles down somewhat, graduates from university or an apprenticeship and gets a responsible job. This represents a major shift in their consciousness and is evidence of much personal growth.

The aim of the game is to grow into an adult, not remain as a child or adolescent. The next trap however is to get stuck in the system. While it is definitely a big deal to step up as an adult and land a decent job when you were fresh out of school or university, if you are still in the same place 20 years later, major problems start arising.

Working as an employee in the system (level 4) is all about making someone else rich and serving someone else's vision. To do that requires suppressing your own great ideas and just doing what you are told. Initially, to submit to leadership represents significant growth when you are young, but now that you have a few of your own grey hairs it is time for you to start leading rather than being a follower for the rest of your life.

While each of the 7 levels are essential and healthy in the beginning, the longer you stay there, the unhealthier it becomes and the more pain you will experience. At mid-life, it is a common experience to no longer be enjoying your job. However, this pain is a gift that serves you to finally take the step of doing your own thing and exploring your own entrepreneurial vision.

This is why the step in growing from system (level 4) to entrepreneur (level 5) is almost entirely about personal development. You've got to face your fears, get clear about what you really want in life, decide if you have anything of value to offer the world and be prepared to embrace uncertainty and back yourself.

The Framework

*To solve any problem all you need is the proven framework
and someone skilful enough to hold you in the space until
you get the results you are after.*

Left unaddressed insecurity can only lead to madness.

There is a clear, intelligent and complete solution.
The aim of the game is to be fully human.
It is to be alive and unhindered.
To be moving forward into the things you deeply desire without
the handbrake on.
It is to be able to show up as the best version of yourself in
the real world totally present and unguarded with nothing to
prove and defend.
It is to create a life that you don't need an escape from.
It is to operate with power and grace in the world.
It is to live your life the way you really know you are capable
of and by doing so, to leave your mark on the planet.
It is to live out of a story that is beautiful, expansive and full of
empowering beliefs

"Success leaves clues"
ANTHONY ROBBINS

There are many people who have found a way to show up in life unhindered by self-doubt, limiting beliefs and the fear of not being good enough. They have not just managed their insecurity they have overcome it. My work has been to observe how they did it. If they can do it, I can do it. If I can do it, you can do it.

In every case, whether they were explicitly aware of it or not, these seven practices showed up consistently. They didn't win against insecurity because they were better, stronger or smarter than the average punter; they did it by practising all seven things. These seven practices are all that made the difference. Seven simple and hard things that most people would never apply to their life, but if they did, they too would find the way to live unhindered by insecurity.

My work has been to make these seven practices as explicit and clear as possible. You do not need to recreate the wheel. The insecurity problem has already been solved successfully by all kinds of people. If you too would like to be able to show up at your best where it matters most, free from the nagging, debilitating fear that somehow you are going to get found out as not being good enough, these seven practices will work for you too.

Solving the insecurity problem will cause you to become

unhindered. Being unhindered will inevitably lead you to explore new worlds of possibility and take you into unchartered waters. Stepping into increasing uncertainty will expose new levels of insecurity. At each new stage of growth there will be opportunities to cycle through all seven levels again as you are exposed to new challenges, fears and uncertainties.

Insecurity can be overcome because it has been overcome. This is not a new problem and you are not special. Your insecurity is not somehow different or more difficult. This is a universal fear, which makes it an entirely predictable problem with a predictable solution.

Let's delve into the seven essential practices for overcoming insecurity.

Practice 1:
Step into the light

Until you are fully here, you can never begin
the process of getting there.

The first essential practice for overcoming insecurity is to step into the light. It's the access point into the other seven stages. The gateway to change. The beginning of the journey. It is what makes all the other stages possible.

Name your fear

It is really common to feel insecure about being insecure. I get it. Yet, at some point, you've got to face up to the fact that you are insecure. Whether you want to be or not, whether you should be or not, the truth is you are. You are here. Until you accept that, lasting change is not even an option.

Stage one in this epic and beautiful work you are about to undertake is to stop running, step into the light and name your fear. The only way out is through. There is no other way around it.

Winning a boxing world championship starts with calling out an opponent.

> *You...the one with the big head and flat nose. I want to fight you.*

You can't train, prepare or win if you don't even know who you are fighting.

If you think your battle is against your behaviour, you are wrong. If you think you need to fight what others have said about you, you are mistaken. If you want to punch on with your dysfunctional patterns of emotion and thought, you're in the wrong weight division. The opponent you seek is your own opinion of yourself. It is the fear of inadequacy, the deep uncertainty about whether you are enough.

"Named must your fear be, before banish it you can"
YODA

This is the main event. Nothing else matters.

Be precise in your speech

Jordan Peterson[7] teaches that specificity turns chaos into a thing that you can deal with. If you have a vague unease, you will struggle with it until you define it explicitly and give it a concrete form. He says that it is essential to be precise in your speech.

> *"Problems that go unnamed become*
> *monsters that consume you"*
> JORDAN PETERSON

Each of these seven practices are essential for overcoming insecurity. That means fully embracing every one of them. To resist or semi-apply allows insecurity to remain. In the first practice I understand that awareness, honesty and vulnerability is hard, but I didn't make these rules, I'm simply explaining them to you.

Hiding is natural, stepping into the light goes against our self-preservation instincts. Nevertheless, if you'd like to eradicate insecurity from your life, there is no other way. One of the most important aspects of turning the lights on and being here starts with the language we use to describe where here is.

Here are two examples of imprecise descriptions that keep

---

7   I'm convinced this guy is the smartest man on the planet now, and one of the most important voices of our generation. Rule 10 of Jordan Peterson's *12 Rules for Life* is to be precise in your speech. You've got to read this book. (or at least listen to the audio version...) Jordan Peterson, *12 rules for life, and antidote to chaos,* Random House Canada, 2018.

people in the dark and therefore outside of their transformation process.

The imposter syndrome

One of the most common questions I get asked is whether the imposter syndrome and the insecurity problem are the same thing. I also have people frequently tell me that they are not insecure at all but often battle the imposter monster when they step out of their comfort zone.

As with all labels, they provide a level of distance between the person themselves and the thing that describes what they are struggling with. This distance always disempowers the person's ability to change their experience. Labels are imprecise. They are massive generalisations and abstractions that take on a life of their own.

> *I have an anxiety disorder.*

> *I've got depression.*

> *I'm an introvert.*

> *I'm a people pleaser.*

> *There is this thing happening to me externally that I have no control over.*

The moment you say that you struggle with the imposter

syndrome, you lose all ability to win. You can fight against it, but you can never defeat it because you do not control it. The label makes you a victim. And being a victim leaves you without power.

The value of this victimhood is that it provides a culturally accepted excuse as to why you have not achieved your potential. This is why many people choose to cling to it rather than move to a more precise description of the real problem.

Let's take a moment to deconstruct the imprecise language of the imposter syndrome. To be an imposter is to present a false image that hides the truth of who you really are. It is to be a fraud or a fake. The imposter is a pretender. They do not belong. They do not deserve their seat at the table. They have tricked or manipulated their way in. Therefore, the imposter is only ever a moment away from being exposed and found out.

The word 'syndrome' takes something abstract and makes it real. It quantifies the generalisation and gives substance to the thing it describes. To add syndrome to imposter makes the feeling more concrete and less changeable at the same time.

It's a syndrome? Oh, so it's actually a thing.

The imposter syndrome is simply the abstract generalisation of feeling as though you are about to be found out. You are afraid that you are moments away from being exposed as somehow inadequate, lacking value, or bad. It's exactly the same thing as the insecurity problem. Calling it the imposter syndrome/ monster insulates you from having to face your fear, but also means you can never overcome your fear.

Failure and rejection

When I begin to facilitate open and honest dialogue about a person's fears, it is typical for them to stop a few layers short. In their awareness of what they are most afraid of, most people imagine that it is either the fear of failure or the fear of rejection (or both) that hinder them the most. However, while this awareness may feel incredibly honest and raw, it is entirely useless. In fact, describing fear in this way makes it impossible to overcome.

Imagine for a moment that were true. You're right. Your deepest insecurity is the fear of failure. Now what? What are you supposed to do with that information?

The only way to protect yourself from that fear is to never try in the first place. Clearly that is not a tenable solution. There are a multitude of very successful people who fail regularly! Perhaps only 1 in 5 of their big ideas actually work. Yet this failure has never stopped them succeeding.

The same logic applies to the fear of rejection. The only way to avoid being rejected is to never put yourself out there. Never do anything that is different or obsess about pleasing every single person you know at all times for the rest of your life.

Obviously, this is not a believable plan. The reason neither of these options provide genuine solutions is because neither failure nor rejection are the problem in the first place.

The deepest level of fear is always the personal implications of these things instead. Here is the high-quality question for stepping into the light and being precise with your fear: And if that were to happen, (i.e. you were to fail or be rejected) what would that say about you?

Now it is personal. The implications of failure would go beyond the fact that you've failed and highlight that you *are* a failure. The personal implications of being rejected are that you are not deserving of love. There must be something wrong with you. Failure and rejection have simply exposed you to what you are actually afraid of. You are concerned there is something inadequate, lacking or bad about you.

Your own opinion of you

Practice one centres around being incredibly precise about exactly what you are afraid of. This point cannot be over-stated. You are not afraid of failure — you are afraid of what you think failure would say about you. You are not afraid of being rejected — it is the implications of what rejection says about your value and worth.

This fear is the insecurity of being found out as not being good enough. Even more precise, therefore, is your own opinion of yourself that scares you the most. This means you are not afraid of what others think of you, you are actually afraid of what *you* think of you.

Your
Own
Opinion
Of
You.

> *"There is no value-judgment more important to man—no factor more decisive in his psychological development and motivation—than the estimate he passes on himself."*
> NATHANIEL BRANDEN

There will be a thousand opportunities to shut down this level of awareness and move the problem back up the levels of abstraction, but every time you step away from this level of laser precision you step out of the seven essential practices framework. Once again you will be stuck.

The word 'opinion' changes everything even without you changing anything. Opinion is never used to describe that which is concrete, true, objectively verifiable, or universally accepted. Instead it is used to describe a thought or belief you have about something or someone.

The dictionary defines the word opinion as:

A belief or judgment that rests on grounds insufficient to produce complete certainty.

A personal view, attitude, or appraisal not necessarily based on fact or knowledge.

For example: "That, in my opinion, is right."

This means that the problem you are trying to fix is not you. You are not the problem. It is just your opinion of you. You on the other hand are working perfectly.

Awareness

If you have any chance of dealing with the madness causing insecurity inside you, it all starts with awareness. You cannot change what you cannot see. While ever you continue to fight surface level problems rather than deal with the deepest level problem, you'll keep running around in circles.

Lasting change starts with you being willing to come out of hiding and face up to your current reality. It requires a level of acceptance and honesty about what is really going on in your life that most people will never have the courage to own up to. Fear largely exists on the level of imagination and abstraction. When it is left unexamined, not only does this fear continue, but it continues to grow. Every moment spent observing our fear weakens it.

The dispassionate observer

When a person begins to reflect on their own behaviour in an attempt to increase self-awareness, often they do it as the critic or the drill sergeant. They imagine that shaming themselves, disapproving or trying to force themselves to toughen up and just get it sorted will bring about change. Yet the internal critic, or the drill sergeant, never brings about lasting change because they come from a place of judgment. This causes us to shut down and hide which further suppresses our stuff.

One of the best ways to reflect on your own life is as a dis-passionate observer. That means you have no agenda, no judgement, and no opinion. You are simply curious.

You can't do awareness and self-judgement at the same time

To have clear self-awareness and be judging yourself at the same time is literally impossible. In the presence of judgment, it is not safe to be honest. You can't afford to turn all the lights on and reveal the truth of the situation in case that truth reveals something bad or wrong about you.

Newtonian physics says that every action has an equal and opposite reaction. With this in mind, judgment creates defen-siveness. Judgment says there is right and wrong, good and bad, so be careful not to make a mistake. When questions are asked that have the potential to expose you, you can't afford to give an honest answer. You need to give the correct answer instead.

In order to do genuine self-awareness, whatever you discover has to be OK. If there is any potential to implicate yourself by exploring your true self, then the instinct for self-preservation will take over and all examination will be shut down.

Self-judgment

One of the heaviest, most unproductive things we carry in life is self-judgement. People are often so much harder on themselves than anyone else. In order to dial down the judgment, the key is to deconstruct and understand the intention of self-judgement as a strategy. You are never going to stop judging yourself by judging yourself for judging yourself. That one is a hard loop to break out of!

Contrary to popular opinion, the purpose of self-judgement is not to make you try harder or be better (like the drill sergeant). The purpose of self-judgement is actually a pre-emptive strike. We fear the judgment of others, so we get in first and beat ourselves down so that if and when others do, it doesn't hurt as much.

Self-judgement is therefore all about self-protection. Interestingly we only protect that which we value. The more value we place on something or someone, the more motivated we are to keep them safe. As it turns out, we protect ourselves for the same reason. Not because we are trying to ruin our lives, but from a place of deep love. If you really didn't care about yourself, it makes no sense to be investing so much energy in playing it safe.

Self-judgment = Self-protection = Self-love.

Now, knowing the intention, I'm sure you could find more resourceful ways of loving yourself than being so self-critical.

Be Here

A central theme within the first practice of turning the lights on is to be here. If you were to open Google maps and enter your desired destination, Google would require your starting location before being able to give you a road map. If you have privacy settings protecting your current location from being discovered, getting directions to where you want to go becomes impossible.

I see this very thing happen all the time when people set goals. They are clear about where they want to be, but unclear about their exact starting point. They don't want to be *here*...they just want to be *there*! It's common to be embarrassed, disappointed, frustrated, annoyed and ashamed about the current set up. Therefore, who wants to focus on that? Can we just not focus on *here*, and keep visualising *there*? Please? Surely that will work.

The point is, that clearly cannot work. You've got to be *here* before you can get *there*. Being frustrated is natural but I promise you it is not helping you change your reality. All change work requires the ability to see clearly what it is you are changing. And you can't change it if you can't see it.

Practice one is all about dialling down the self-judgment, coming out of hiding and fully showing up *here* — wherever *here* may be. This is the time to become crystal clear about the state of play in your health, relationships, finances, work, confidence level and beliefs. It is the time for brutal honesty and ownership of all your current results, not to be projecting about the results you are hoping for. Ultimately being here is to give an exact representation of your current position. The good, the bad and the ugly.

Face up or run away

Psychotherapist Nathaniel Branden explains just how essential this practice really is in his ground-breaking book *The Psychology of Self-Esteem*. Branden teaches that each new day provides us with a central choice as to how we will orient our life. We can either face up to the challenges, opportunities, dilemmas, conflict and problems that life brings, or we can run away. This central choice then has significant consequences that ultimately shape our self-esteem.

The choice to run away is often cloaked in various forms of self-deception so as to not appear to be just giving up or taking the easy path. It may show up as blame, excuse, avoidance, procrastination, obfuscation, pretending, game playing or even self-sabotage.

Obviously, it is possible to get out of doing things you are not comfortable with or afraid of, yet you do not escape scot-free. While you may successfully get out of the situation, you take emotional baggage with you as a result of running away. When your head hits the pillow at night, running away leaves you with residual shame, guilt and anxiety.

As we are sense-making creatures, the unconscious meaning we give to our running away experience, is that we don't have what it takes to deal with life. We teach ourselves that running is the only way to deal with hard things. The pattern is reinforced with each new experience until the learning is deeply embedded. This leaves people with the distinct belief that they are not good enough, that they can't cope, and they form the opinion that there is something inadequate about them.

As stated above, this can only lead to an incredibly low sense of self and very poor self-esteem. On the other hand, if the alternate choice is made, and the governing principle for one's life becomes to face up instead, the consequence is dramatically different.

Although facing up is much more difficult, this path yields far better results when it comes to our self-esteem. To face up to life may also be described as: To confront, accept, own, deal with, decide, or resolve. Although the challenge may be great and the path unfamiliar, facing up to life means we bring our best effort to what is in front of us. The often-surprising discovery in these moments of difficulty is that our best proves to be enough. We somehow make it through without being overcome.

It turns out these experiences, although difficult, leave us with very different emotions than when the choice is made to run away. Instead of shame guilt and anxiety we feel confidence, strength and peace. Those who face up sleep considerably better than those who run away.

In the process of facing up, we discover that we are stronger than first thought. The meaning placed on these experiences is that this success reference point says something good about our capacity to handle whatever life throws our way. This opinion leads to a strong belief in our inherent value and worth as a person. Ultimately, this is Branden's suggested path towards a healthier self-esteem.

The psychology of self-esteem

	FACE UP	RUN AWAY
Alternate definition	Own, accept, responsibility, confront, deal with, stand, honesty	Blame, excuse, procrastinate, obfuscate, avoid, pretend, hide, lie
Emotional state	Strength, confidence, peace	Shame, guilt, anxiety
Teach yourself	You have what it takes to deal with life, you are stronger than you thought	You don't have what it takes to deal with life, you need to keep running, you are weak
Believe	You are enough	You are not enough
Self esteem	High	Low

To embrace practice number one therefore will require you to stop running and start facing up to life. Whether you should be here or not is abstract and irrelevant. You *are* here. Whether you should have a low opinion of yourself or poor self-esteem is a pointless enquiry. The point is you do fear that you are not good enough. Practice one requires you to stop lying to yourself and others and to stop pretending not to know what is true.

After being introduced to this concept by my former business partner Robert Holmes, [8] I can still vividly remember the first time I used it in a coaching conversation with a client. It had been 2 weeks since our first session as part of a two-month arrangement which entitled her to unlimited coaching. After checking in to see how she was travelling, she explained that things were difficult and that she had reconsidered whether this was in fact the best time to be diving into a deep change process. In her mind it seemed that everything was conspiring against her and due to the pressures of her life situation, she was not devoting enough time to working through the content and frameworks I'd set as homework.

She explained that due to her current situation it was probably best to stop our coaching sessions until things settled down. I listened to all she had to say and then took the opportunity to explain Branden's self-esteem model. From her backstory that

---

8   Robert and I formerly ran Frazer Holmes coaching together. Robert now leads the team at Neuro Coaching Australia. Credit must also go to my former business associate Sue Hefren who summarised Nathaniel Branden's very academic book, into a practical framework our team of coaches could use. Nathaniel Branden, *The psychology of self-esteem,* Jossey Bass, 1969

she'd shared in our first session, it was apparent that her whole life had been a series of running away experiences. Every time challenges arose, she would deal with the feelings of being overwhelmed by giving up, walking away, or hiding behind a convenient excuse. She had trained everyone in her world to treat her as a fragile porcelain doll, and as such, friends and family helped her run away by buying into her excuses.

I explained this pattern to her and could sense the deep impact it was having as she came to terms with the reality of it. I told her that she was welcome to the decision to postpone our sessions, yet as her coach, my role was to serve her to get more of what she wanted.

The very reason she had enlisted me to help her in the first place was to overcome insecurity and resolve the self-esteem issues that had constantly hindered her experience of life. The psychology of self-esteem shows definitively that the reason her opinion of herself was so low was due to her reluctance to face up to life and to run away the moment things got hard instead.

I told her that to help solve the self-esteem issue, and at the same time allow her to run away from the coaching agreement, cancelled each other out! The irony was not lost on her.

So, what are you going to do?

I really understand what you are saying about

self-esteem. That totally makes sense, so I'll need to set aside some time to really think about it this week.

Rubbish. You don't need any time to think. You'll just run away again. Make a decision now. What are you going to do?

Hmmm...You're right. I'm just scared. Ok, I'm not going to run away.

Don't tell me what you are not going to do, what are you committing to?

Wow. This is so hard! Ok, I'm in...All in. I'm going ahead with this coaching process even though things are hard right now.

No more porcelain doll?

No more fragile princess.

Good for you. We are back on track. I'll call you tomorrow.

The whole conversation lasted no more than 10 minutes, but her life was never the same again. In that moment of aware-ness and courage, she entered into a new way of living. The path of transformation had instantly become open.

The handbrake is on

While this negative opinion of yourself still exists inside you, you will never have permission to succeed. The handbrake is firmly on.

Equipped with this awareness of the real problem, the way forward is not to force yourself to do that which you don't want to do, but to fully understand how this internal resistance is actually driven by love to protect you from what you fear. When you overcome the fear and refocus the love, there is nothing that could stop you from moving forward.

The common path

The truth is that most people will never even arrive at stage one in this process. They are insecure about being insecure and so they feel the need to keep running away from their fear. The thought of turning to face the thing that most terrifies them is a bridge too far.

Due to the fear of being found out as inadequate, people protect themselves by projecting an image of success. If they appear to have it all together then maybe no one will ever suspect that they don't. There is too much at stake to stop now and review their whole operation. Too much has been invested in the image they project to the world. They've got to keep up the appearance of success and smooth over the cracks.

However, while stepping into the light is incredibly vulnerable and courageous, there is no other way to deal with fear. Practice one sets the stage for the drama to unfold.

The essence of practice 1 – Step into the light:

Be here – You can't get there until you know where you are starting from. Whether you should be here or shouldn't be here is irrelevant. Here is where you are. It's time to let your guard down, come out of hiding and give an accurate assessment about the state of play.

Turn the lights on – Insecurity is built on a work of fiction that only survives when left unexamined. You can't change what you can't see. Awareness is crucial to all change work.

Be precise – Define the exact problem you are dealing with. The deepest level of fear is always your own opinion of yourself. The surface level pain in your health, finances, work, relationships and sense of purpose are just symptoms of the real problem.

Face up to your reality – Every time you run away you undermine your own self esteem. It's time to face up and move towards a healthy sense of self instead.

Judgement free space – Approach your own situation with curiosity and compassion without judgment. You can't do self-awareness and self-judgment at the same time.

Practice 2:
100% Responsibility

Everything changes the moment you realise you are already 100% responsible for your results.

The second essential practice for overcoming insecurity is to let go of all blame and excuse and take 100% responsibility for your life.

A work of fiction

Once someone comes to terms with the fact that there is deep insecurity limiting them, and that their opinion of themselves is the real problem they are trying to solve, the next logical step is to go looking at *why* they would have such a low opinion of themselves.

Typically, people go back to moments of pain, loss, disappointment, hurt and abuse caused by others to answer this question. Yep, it all makes sense. You're insecure because of what was said and done to you, or not said and done to you. But it is what it is. You can't change the past. They are then left in a worse place then when they started the process. All that awareness has just increased the pain in their life without giving them any ability to change the story. Thankfully, that is *not* how it actually works.

In overcoming my own insecurity, the single most important idea was this: *All insecurity is built on a work of fiction.* I imagined that I felt inadequate and insecure because of all the negative things said and done to me. In my mind these experiences proved that there was something lacking inside me or that I was somehow not enough. Yet, the game-changing discovery was that life is not about what happens to us, it is about the *meaning* we place on these things.

Sense making creatures

That one thought changes everything. It immediately took me out of the victim space into a place of personal power. It turns out I didn't feel insecure because of the sum total of things that had happened to me, I felt inadequate because of the story I told myself about what each of these experiences meant about me. I created my own insecurity! It only existed in my head!

Our brain filters all possibilities to simply find more evidence for whatever we believe is true. So, perception becomes reality. In every single event, experience and conversation we have, our subconscious mind is asking and answering two powerful questions to make sense of our situation:

- Why did that just happen?
- What does it mean about me?

More often than not, the answers to these questions are negative and self-depreciating. We naturally assume negative events are in some way a reflection of our own value and worth. Once we make these kinds of decisions around meaning, this information becomes the foundation for all beliefs and becomes the story we live out of for the rest of our lives. Our brain filters all possibilities to simply find more evidence for whatever we believe is true. So, perception becomes reality.

Agreements

In his best-selling book *The Four Agreements*[9], author Don Miguel Ruiz reveals that our life is not shaped by the experiences we have, but by the agreements we make. This is a profound insight that means no one has the power to bless or curse us without our permission.

Often people have words spoken to them or about them playing on repeat in their head sometimes decades after they were first delivered. It seems these create a person's destiny for good or bad. However, it is not the words spoken to us or about us that bless or curse us, only the words we agree with.

---

9   I had a profoundly spiritual experience reading this book on a flight to Melbourne. I am certain it represents genuine wisdom and is a must read. Don Miguel Ruiz, *The 4 Agreements, A Toltec Wisdom Book,* Amber-Allen Publishing, California, 1997.

The reason why those words changed your life is because you decided they were true. You agreed. This discovery is at the core of practice 2 – taking 100% responsibility for your life.

Wait...What?! I thought my life was ruined as a 5-year-old when my dad told me I was stupid!

Nope. That is not how life works.

Think about the flip side of this for a moment. If parents had the ability to automatically install beliefs in their children simply by what they said to them, then every mummy's boy who'd been told how special they were would naturally go on to change the world.

If you were to review the data of all the words spoken to you, and about you, as a child, it is likely that there were far more positive and encouraging things said than negative ones. If it was just about the words, then most people would be totally confident and comfortable being themselves. (Note to readers: most people are NOT confident and comfortable.)

The game changer here is that it is not about the words. It never has been. It is about our agreement with those words. You decided it was true and so it was. You could also decide it was not true and so would not be. Well, what about the things you have no control over, like agreements made for you without choice?

Society tells me that a woman must look a certain way to be accepted. She must also put her family before her career. If she wants to succeed in the work/business space, she won't be treated or paid as an equal to her male counterparts.

Surely, that is what it is? Well only if you agree. 'Yeah but if I disagree who cares. Everyone else agrees it is true, so I have to fight their agreements.' I'm not suggesting there won't be opposition, but there are multitudes of examples of women who never signed off on this 'societal agreement' and lived by very different rules.

It is only true for you if you say it is. No one has the ability to take power from you; it is only ever given away.

Blame and excuse

Blame feels too good to let go of. It makes so much sense to be upset at those who've caused you grief in life and to feel that the villains in your life have affected you. Blame is fair. No one can blame you for blaming. The point is, that the things that have happened to you ARE unfair. They ARE wrong. You are right! However, while you are totally justified in your blame, and your excuse is valid, it just gives you zero power to change anything.

You are not a victim

The central focus of practice two is to realise this is not actually about taking 100% responsibility, it is to see that you are already responsible – whether you like it or not. The more you grasp this idea, blaming others stops making sense all together.

111

When you try it on, it no longer fits. You catch yourself in the mirror and laugh at how ridiculous it looks on you now.

You are not a victim. You have never been the victim. While you may not have chosen what happens to you, you always get to choose your response. Therefore, you are exactly where you have chosen to be. To take this idea all the way to its logical conclusion shows that not only are you far from the victim you once imagined, you are in fact the bully in this situation! You are the one who has said and done the unkind things to yourself. You are the one who has been critical, negative and self-depreciating.

Change always comes out of responsibility. It is essential and inescapable. Your results are yours. Your relationships are yours. Your life is yours. You are the only one with the power to hold yourself back and the only one with the power to set yourself free. It is all you. Everything changes the moment you realise you *are* already 100% responsible for your results.

Secondary gain

To practice 100% responsibility effectively, you'll need to cut up your victim card and forfeit all of the accrued benefits and frequent flier points. To come to terms with and fully apply the concept of secondary gain to your life is still one of the most 'make or break' aspects of lasting change. This is often the hardest and most offensive piece of the puzzle to explain.

So central is this principle in facilitating lasting change, most nights it shows up in my dreams! I often find myself going to great lengths to talk this though with those looking for change even when I'm asleep! Here are how these conversations play out:

I'm frustrated that I have no clarity.

How's having no clarity working for you?

It's not. I get nothing out of it. My head is just always so messy and unclear.

Oh...What if having no clarity means you never have to take any decisive action which means you can't ever get it wrong. No clarity protects you from failure, risk and disappointment. You could actually have clarity the moment you'd like it.

*   *   *

I'm so sick of having no money.

How's being broke working for you?

It's not. There are absolutely no benefits of being poor.

Are you sure?

Yep.

In Australia, with a decent education and an able body, you are still poor?

Hmmm...Interesting.

So, what is dangerous about having money then? What fears would that expose you to? What would you have to go do or who would you have to be if you had no financial restraints?

How about these great benefits?

You get to complain about how unfair big business is, how corrupt the government is, how much of a sell out your friends and family are, you can wave your finger at the corruption in the world and take the moral high ground.

You never have to see what you'd be like with money. Would it corrupt you too? Could you be trusted? Would you become greedy and selfish? Would others then be judging you the way you are judging them?

* * *

Everyone in my family takes me for granted. My whole life revolves around doing what everyone else wants me to.

How's it working for you to be treated so poorly?

It's not. I absolutely hate it. It makes me so sad.

How long has it been like this?

20 years.

Wow! Must be working incredibly well for you to have tolerated this for so long! It would be entirely impossible to wake up each new day and do it all again if there were zero benefits or rewards. We only do what works.

How about this list of great payoffs?

- You get to be the martyr, which means you are the best person you know. You get to tell yourself how wonderful you are because of what you sacrifice for others and for how much pain you can tolerate and then turn the other cheek. You are basically a saint.
- You get self pity and pity from others every time you tell your story.
- You can't fail at going last.
- Others need you and depend on you, which means you must have value.
- You never have to put yourself out there and risk being found out as somehow inadequate.

115

This is what makes responsibility so damn hard. Being the victim fuels some people's whole existence and identity, which makes it incredibly difficult to let go of. Playing the victim card is one of the most effective and excellent strategies for hiding and being safe. The victim card works so much better than Flybuys, or Qantas points. There are so many great benefits of being the victim, it is so hard to cut up that card and forfeit all your accrued points. Without responsibility, none of this is your fault. You can point the finger at someone or something else.

> *'Hey look...I'd so love to do all kinds of great things with my life, but I can't. All the people who've hurt, damaged, abused, lied to, stolen from, and bullied me have taken my chance from me. If none of this had happened, I'd be fine. But it did happen, and I'm not fine. So, it's out of my hands.'*

Whatever you tolerate, and or complain about, but don't change MUST be working for you. That is human psychology 1-0-1. The things we tolerate but don't change always protect us from what we are most afraid of! That is, being exposed as somehow inadequate or not good enough.

As you can imagine, when the fear is gone, there is no longer any reason to tolerate what you don't want. You can take the power back the moment you are willing to part with the payoff you got for giving it away in the first place.

Your results are exactly as you've created them to be

There is a really beautiful insight from the world of NLP (Neuro linguistic programming) that people work perfectly. This is another key idea introduced in my last book *Elegantly Simple Solutions to Complex People Problems* that demands to be part of this insecurity conversation as well.

Your behaviour is not nearly as weird, broken, messy, or random as you think. Behaviour is simply the end of the assembly line produced by the factory of your beliefs. What's more, your behaviour never lies. It is an incredibly accurate representation of your beliefs. People think they believe all kinds of wonderful things, but what must you believe in order to behave that way?

If you see that your behaviour is part of a well-constructed system, it takes all the mystery out of the process of self-awareness. System thinking turns the work of personal transformation into a clear scientific process. If our behaviour is a system, then there must be a design. If there is a design, then there is a strategy. If there is a strategy, there is an intention. If there is an intention, it can be observed. If it can be observed, it can be deconstructed. If it can be deconstructed, it can be changed. If it can be changed, it can be improved and reconstructed!

Of course, and you love this!

Of course, you are stuck, broke, unhappy, anxious, depressed, lonely, and/or overweight. What's the problem? That's the exact result you've designed your system to produce. At some point in time, to solve a problem or meet a need, you've created a strategy, designed a system and built a process to get you a clear result. Often that strategy is built around avoiding pain, being safe, or protecting yourself from what you are most afraid of. The point is, it is still working the way you designed it to. And it will continue to keep producing the same results until you change the blinkin' thing. Of course!

There is no judgment here, but this system is not broken. To take this even further, part of you loves the exact results you are producing right now. When you are willing to stop pretending your results are such a mystery and start examining the system you have lovingly created for yourself, you give yourself an incredible amount of power to change these very results. You love this. If you didn't, you would have already changed it.

People
Work
Perfectly.

You already *are* responsible.

Anxiety is a great example of this. Did you know that anxiety needs a story in order to survive? Contrary to popular opinion, anxiety is not a condition that you simply have to survive or endure. It doesn't come out of nowhere. You are not broken. What's more, the source of your anxiety is not strange, random or unknown. There is always a reason, an underlying belief, a fear or insecurity that has created the anxiety response to something in your reality. Of course you are anxious. What did you expect? That is the only emotional state you could possibly be in right now. Emotion always flows out of belief.

If there was no limiting belief, then it just doesn't make any sense to be anxious. What must you believe about your life, your situation or yourself in order to be anxious? Clearly part of you must feel in some way inadequate, incapable or that you are not up to the challenge in front of you, otherwise it would be impossible to feel anxious.

You don't feel anxious about tying your shoelace or eating your breakfast because there is zero doubt in your mind that you know how to do this. You've done these things thousands of times before and you know this time will be no different. The point is anxiety is not random. It flows out of the story you are living out of. It simply reveals what you believe to be true in any one moment.

What would you need to believe right now in order to be feeling calm, confident and in control of your results? Those who are living free from anxiety – what must they believe? Therefore, the aim of the game is to live out of a story where to be anxious makes no sense.

Now is your chance to re-write that story.

No one is coming to save you

When people feel that their insecurity was created outside of them, they go looking outside of themselves for it to be fixed. When you realise you created this mess, then you also realise you are the only one who can fix it. You start looking inside instead. No one is coming to save you. This is absolutely brutal but wonderfully empowering at the same time.

This is all about you

The key here is to trace your deepest fear all the way back to what you fear about yourself, rather than what you fear about what others may say or do to you.

The thing is, you are not actually afraid of being rejected, failing or not being loved. It is what these events or experiences would say about you if they were to happen that terrifies you the most. Therefore, you are actually afraid of your own thoughts about yourself. You fear you are not enough, so it is your own opinion you are actually terrified of. This is ALL about you.

Interestingly, this is actually really good news. While ever you think this is about someone else then you give all your power away and have to wait for others to fix this for you through kindness, generosity or love. Yet what if these things never come your way? What if the people in your world are incapable of giving you these things?

The most amazing realisation is that even when love is given, until you believe you are worth loving, you will filter it out anyway. It turns out the only opinion that matters is yours. Until you take full responsibility to change your own opinion of yourself, you will live as a victim to this fear for the rest of your life. Responsibility puts you in the power position.

The four stages of transformation

Mindset transformation experts Brian Grasso and Carrie Campbell describe the process of lasting change using the four A's. [10]

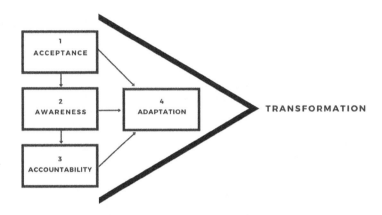

Stage 1. Acceptance

Transformation starts with specifically accepting that all we have is story. We are sense making creatures who go into the world and tell stories about our experiences. We don't see reality, just our perception of reality. In every experience we have, subconsciously we are asking and answering these 2 questions: Why did this happen?; and what does it mean about me? The answers to these questions become the basis for the stories we live out of.

---

10 Adapted from The 4 A's model developed by Brian Grasso and Carrie Campbell. http://www.brianandcarrie.live

Stage 2. Awareness

If all we have is story, what awareness do you have of the specific story are you living out of and its origin? Everything is created twice. Your current results are merely the by-product of the script you've been living out of. Awareness is essential because if you can't see it, you can't change it.

Stage 3. Accountability

This stage is about being accountable to the fact that you are not the actor in the story, you are the storyteller. Transformation happens as you hold yourself accountable to 100% choice and responsibility. You are not a victim and you get to choose your story. The question then becomes: what story would you like to live out of? Keep choosing the new story. Keep choosing empowering meaning on the defining moments of your life.

Stage 4. Adaptation

This stage is simply the fruit of doing the first three stages well. Do three stages and you get the fourth one for free! You cannot not experience different results. Behaviour, emotion and thought is at the end of the assembly line of the factory of beliefs. Once you make different choices in the moment and don't give the old patterns any energy, your stories will naturally change. Your results will adapt to follow your new thoughts.

Lasting transformation

The process of personal change always follows a similar path. People often imagine that their issues are somehow more complicated than others or totally unique to them, and there-fore there would need to be a creative solution to solve their problem that was so complex and unique.

Thankfully this is not even close to being accurate. While there may be unique circumstances or experiences in our lives, they are always similar in the kinds of problems they represent. There are common patterns, themes, and challenges we all face as part of what it means to be a human being.

Therefore, the way forward is also common. There is a clear and well-worn path to freedom that has stood the test of time. Your issues are not outside the scope of this common path and so your transformation journey will not actually be unique. (Sorry about that.)

As you step out of the myopic view of your own story and see the big picture patterns and processes, you are then able to take responsibility for doing the simple yet hard work of setting yourself free. This is one of the essential practices of every single person who has found a way out of their own insecurity.

At this point in the process, we are still setting up the space for you to do the deep change work but there is no heavy lifting required yet. Facing your fears and slaying the dragon as the true hero in the story comes later. For now, it is simply about owning the fact that you are the storyteller in this drama not the actor.

It is important to not rush ahead and seek to rewrite your story until everything is set up and ready to go. If you follow these 7 practices in order, there is an inevitability to the process that assures you of lasting change.

Practice 2 is about becoming a responsible adult. It is an invitation to settle down a bit, realise that you are in fact exactly where you have chosen to be and take full responsibility for your part in this mess.

The essence of practice 2 – 100% responsibility:

Let go of blame and excuse – You are well within your rights to be upset at those who've hurt you but blaming them leaves you powerless to improve your situation. When you are ready to hand back the victim card and all its accrued benefits, you are able to move on with your life.

Embrace 100% choice and responsibility — You already *are* responsible. Your results are yours. Your relationships are yours. Your opinion of yourself is yours. You created this mess so you are the only one who can fix it.

You are exactly where you have chosen to be – (and it is working for you). Of course. You love it. Real hope emerges as soon as you break through the illusion of no choice. Realising that insecurity was created internally by you, means you stop looking externally for it to be fixed.

You are the storyteller not just the actor – Our experience of life is not shaped by what happens to us, but by the meaning we place on these things. Therefore, no one has the power to bless or curse us without our permission. You are the one with the pen and paper, and insecurity is a story written by you.

Be at cause not at effect. Be the driver of the bus not a passenger. No one is coming to save you here. It is all you.

Practice 3:
Stack the pain

When the pain of change becomes less than the pain of staying the same, you couldn't stay here even if you wanted to.

The third essential practice for overcoming insecurity is to increase the amount of pain you feel as a result of the insecurity problem. This is called stacking the pain.

Pain is a gift

Pain is designed to lovingly protect us from ruining our lives. Its intention is to keep us safe and improve the quality of our life. Every cell in our body is hardwired to alert us to danger and then move us away from that danger towards safety. If something hurts us physically or emotionally, pain is the body's way of saying 'Hey can you please stop doing that?!'

My son once tearfully told me that I had hurt his feelings. He explained that he knew it was his feelings that had been hurt because he could feel it in his throat.

126

Pain shows us what is important and where our personal boundaries lie. It lets us know when something is wrong and is of great value to us. Without its signals and warnings, we would have no way of knowing where the danger lies.

Therefore, feeling crap about yourself is supposed to hurt. That's the whole point! That painful feeling is actually a loving voice trying to tell you that you weren't designed to feel that way, so you need to do something about that insecurity before it destroys you! The wise thing to do would be listen to your pain and let it lovingly do its job!

Yet instead of listening to their pain, most people are running away from it instead. Because it feels unpleasant and they don't know what to do with the pain, they end up masking, medicating and avoiding the message it brings. If you are to overcome insecurity in your life, listening to your pain is an essential part of the process.

Why people don't listen to their pain

The only reason anyone would willingly ignore or suppress their pain is due to the fear that listening will make their life harder or worse. Pain is always going to tell you to change something. But what if you can't, or its too hard or too scary to make the change being asked of you?

It's like this:

I'm in pain in my work, but if I listen to my pain it will tell me to quit my job and find something better — but what if this is as good as it gets? What if I end up with no work? What if no one wants to employ me?

I'm in pain in my relationships, but what if I listen to my pain and it tells me to leave this relationship and then I end up all alone? Or what if I have to confront some stuff that only causes me to have to go into battle only to lose?

I'm in pain with my health, but what if my pain tells me to lose weight and be healthier and I fail at that? At least I can't fail at being overweight and unhealthy!

Pain is your most honest and loving voice

The thing about pain, is that it always comes from a place of love. We only protect that which we value, so the self-protection mechanism hardwired into each cell demonstrates how deeply we really do love ourselves.

Therefore, listening to your pain means actually listening to your most honest and loving voice. Pain is not trying to ruin your life; it is trying to move you from danger to safety. Therefore, listening to your pain will always lead you to make better choices even if they are hard. Your unconscious wouldn't ask you to make changes if it wasn't for your good and it didn't think you were capable of doing so.

People who do life well, work with themselves, not against themselves. This actually requires them to stop and listen to what is going on inside. If you are not accustomed to listening to yourself, the best place to start is with pain.

Pleasure and pain

All motivation in life comes out of either avoiding pain or pursuing pleasure. We are either motivated to move away from something we don't want or drawn towards something we do want. All action is in some way driven by these two forces. There is always a measure of both pleasure and pain in everything we do but depending on which is greater will determine our behaviour. The great thing about this, is that we are able to alter these associations simply by what we pay attention to.

Smoking

One of the best ways to bring about change in your life is to adjust your pleasure and pain associations. This is why the government have put grotesque images on cigarette packaging in an attempt to stop people smoking. They are trying to link it with pain rather than pleasure.

Yet, it is largely ineffective because pleasure and pain is all about focus, and it is possible for smokers to simply ignore the packet and focus on the enjoyment they get instead.

Just because something is costing you dearly or killing you slowly doesn't mean you have to pay attention to that fact. Otherwise we would all naturally avoid everything that is bad for us.

In today's world, you'd think it would be almost impossible to be a smoker. Knowing what we do about the severe health risks, not to mention the exorbitant financial costs, it seems incredibly reckless to light up. However, millions of people still smoke every day.

How? Simply because we cannot pay attention to everything. We are constantly choosing what to focus on and bring our attention to. It is possible to ignore one thing all together and focus on something else.

However, if you did stop and pay attention to how much smoking is costing you in every area of your life, it would be impossible to continue. In fact, that is the only way people do quit. It becomes more painful to continue than to give up the habit.

Smoking and insecurity have a lot in common. Both are incredibly dangerous to your health and well being, yet just because that is true, doesn't make people automatically remove these things from their life. It is entirely possible to ignore that fact and continue on as though nothing was wrong. Remember, even though something is killing you doesn't guarantee you have to pay attention to that reality.

To quit smoking and overcome insecurity, therefore requires

you to pay attention to the costs involved in continuing instead. When you do that, the pain of staying the same becomes far greater than the costs involved in changing your life. Increased pain leads to increased motivation. You are then prepared to do whatever it takes to move forward. This is a central idea of practice of stacking the pain.

The essence of stacking the pain, therefore, is to link massive pain to the cost of being insecure. This means to fully weigh the impact of self-limiting beliefs and negative opinions in every area of your life.

The importance of getting angry

As coach, my job is to serve people by holding them in the process until it works for them. Their problems are not complicated and unique, and neither are the solutions. The way forward is always simple and hard and it's entirely predictable. With a high degree of accuracy, I can gauge whether someone is on track to solving the insecurity problem in their life or not.

One of the key things I'm tracking in practice three is the presence and application of anger. Being peeved, annoyed, frustrated, sad, or disappointed at your current situation is never going to be enough pain to make the change. I often hear clients use language like:

Yeah, I really need to...I really should...I'm going to make a plan...I'll give that some serious thought.

This is all evidence that there is still not enough pain. Change would be nice, but it's really hard.

For lasting change to actually happen, especially in the deepest issues in your life, there has to be a very strong emotional drive. Anger is one of the most powerful emotional resources we have. At its core, anger is about injustice. It's intention, therefore, is always around the action needed to right the perceived wrongs.

As you become angry, your brain releases chemicals called catecholamines that cause a burst of energy that can last for several minutes. Your blood pressure rises as blood is sent to your arms and legs readying for physical action. Your attention narrows to the source of your anger alone, and everything else fades into the background. Additionally, adrenaline and noradrenaline are sent into the blood stream which all add to the heightened state of arousal. You are now ready to fight.

This may seem excessive and unnecessary to those who pride themselves on being level-headed, yet this is the kind of internal resolve you will need to connect with to change your opinion of yourself. This is no game. Insecurity is a monster. It will destroy you if you don't find a way to disarm it first.

Threshold moments

If you really want to be free from insecurity, there is no point pretending that being insecure is not really causing you any grief. Now is the time to feel your pain as strongly and deeply as possible. Press into your pain. Listen to the intensity of its message to you. Count the cost. How is insecurity ruining your life? Focus on the long-term implications of not dealing with this fear. Look at people around you who have lost the battle and have sadly become consumed by their insecurity to the point of madness and mental illness.

If you are not desperately driven to get out of this pain for good, you will not have enough motivation to keep moving forward in this process. There must be a line in the sand moment in your life where you are no longer willing to tolerate being held back, robbed and hindered by the fear of not being enough. IT MUST END HERE!

Feel this pain, and let it lovingly serve you as it was designed to do. In doing so, the pain of change becomes less than the pain of staying the same. Then suddenly, you will experience the power of having every cell in your body desperately moving you into the change space rather than fighting to stay the same.

Stack
The
Pain.

No one has ever solved the insecurity problem except from a place of great pain. Stack it and dial it up more and more and more until you can't stand it any longer. Until you are prepared to do whatever it takes to change this for good, you have not stacked enough pain.

Discovering my own insecurity monster

I can still vividly remember the experience of facing my own insecurity for the first time. Making the switch from Pastor to Coach was a momentous change in my life. It was not a move that was encouraged or understood by almost a single person in my world at the time, yet I knew deeply, that it was right.

Day one of the first training intensive in Melbourne was such a profound and life-giving experience, I bounced out of the room at the end of the day all pepped up on Mountain Dew so clear and confident about the direction my life was taking. On the 5km walk back to my hotel room, I called my wife and then my mate and told them boldly about the future I could see. I told them about the book I was finally going to write and how it was going to impact the world.

That night I effortlessly punched out the first chapter of my first book. However, at around 11pm when I finally shut the lid on the laptop, all that energy, passion, clarity and confidence instantly turned to fear, dread, anxiety and what have I just done?! Now I've told two people about this and actually committed to the process of producing this book. What if it's terrible? What if I can't finish it? What if I do finish it and it's terrible? What if no one wants to buy it? What if it's a massive failure? What if I actually have nothing of value to say? What if I get judged and criticised for putting my opinion out there?

The act of stepping out into the unknown and embarking on

this project had instantly uncovered a mountain of fear and insecurity lying dormant deep inside me. The monster had been woken. Such was the ferocity and strength of this fear; I didn't sleep a wink all night. So much anxiety wrapped around my chest it was even hard to breathe.

The prevailing thought on my way to class the next morning was that if I don't find a way to fully overcome this insecurity it would destroy my life. Left unaddressed, this monster will consume all my hopes and dreams and create such mental instability that I will doubt my capacity to perform and achieve in every area of my life.

I knew this insecurity ultimately would cause me to show up at my worst where it mattered most. If I didn't solve the insecurity problem, I may as well kiss all hopes and dreams goodbye now. The pain of that thought alone was enough to drive a deep commitment to do whatever it took to face this fear head on. To either die or come out the other side reborn. That was my threshold moment.

True dangers

People who succeed in life don't simply have more courage and less fear. They just fear different things. Even when they are experiencing the pleasure of achieving their goals, they are still highly motivated to move away from pain.

For example, they may link massive pain to:

- Living an unfulfilled life,
- Dying with the music inside them,
- Not leaving a legacy,
- Having unrealised potential,
- Not achieving things because limiting beliefs held them back.

The aim is not to get through all the pain so you only experience pleasure, it is to continue to allow your pleasure and pain associations to serve you powerfully rather than to resist your growth and progress.

An accurate cost assessment

One of the most effective ways of stacking the pain is by doing an accurate cost assessment in your life. We get to determine our own pleasure and pain associations by the way we analyse the upside and downside of things.

For example, a person may link massive pain to public speaking because they are acutely aware of all the perceived threats involved in being in the spotlight. However, things change for them when they also accurately assess the cost of not speaking in public. For anyone trying to achieve something in life, the advantages of public speaking far outweigh the potential costs. In reviewing the data this way, they are in fact altering their pleasure and pain associations. From this point, they then naturally gravitate towards more public speaking opportunities and find themselves moving away from feeling the need to hide or be silenced.

Likewise, it is common for people to have inadvertently linked massive amounts of pain to change, growth or self-awareness. Therefore, they naturally resist and avoid these things. Yet, if the thought of change feels more painful than staying in your current comfort zone, it is simply evidence of a lack of accurately assessing the cost.

To do an accurate cost assessment of the impact of insecurity involves fully answering these four questions:

1. What is the cost of continuing to run your life with unaddressed insecurity?
2. What are the advantages, benefits and rewards of holding onto insecurity?
3. What are all the costs involved in upgrading your life and making lasting change?
4. What are all the upsides and advantages of change?

Being thorough in this analysis is often difficult to do alone. I find people typically underestimate or totally miss the hidden costs of insecurity.

Here are some of the significant costs that are far harder to see:

- Outsourcing your significance to others leaves you vulnerable. What if people won't give you the recognition or validation you desire?
- Running childish strategies as an adult leaves you ill equipped for the complexity of life. Sure, adulting is hard, but it is harder than it needs to be when you are trying to deal with adult challenges...as the child.
- Broken rapport with self means you are cut off from your internal resourcefulness.
- Operating without permission to shine or succeed is like driving the car with the handbrake on. It is incredibly inefficient and damaging.
- Being the victim leaves you powerless to improve anything.
- Tolerating dysfunctional relationships causes massive loneliness and unhappiness.
- Back foot living means you constantly miss opportunities as life passes you by.
- Neediness leads to hurtfulness.

If you miss all these costs, then you deceive yourself about the impact insecurity is having on your life. Also, if you can't see exactly how it is costing you, then you will certainly not have enough pain to cause you to deal with it.

No pain, no motivation.

No motivation, no change.

This highlights the need to get help from someone who can help you see the things you can't, or don't want to see, yourself. I'll talk more about this in practice five.

Practice 3 dials up the motivation for you to do whatever it takes to face your fear and overcome all insecurity right now.

The essence of practice 3 – stack the pain:

Accurately assess the cost of unresolved insecurity – Just because something is killing you, doesn't mean you have to pay attention to that fact. Otherwise we would naturally avoid the things that are bad for us. Stacking the pain is all about accurately weighing the full impact insecurity is having on your life now and into the future.

Feel the pain of insecurity – Pain is your most honest and loving voice. It is designed to protect you from further pain. Don't mask, medicate or avoid it. This is a journey into pain not away from it.

Create a threshold – The more pain you feel, the more moti-vated you are to take action. Get to the point where the pain of change is less than the pain of staying the same. All those who have successfully overcome insecurity, have done so from a place of great pain.

Let pain serve you – Pain is an essential aspect of all change. Pain is a signal to get your attention; to let you know that some-thing is unaddressed in your life and to motivate you to take necessary action. Listen to your pain and allow it to lead you to a better place.

Practice 4:
Develop a compelling
life vision

The moment you lose sight of the big dream you have for your life, the process of change becomes way too hard.

The fourth essential practice for overcoming insecurity is to develop a compelling life vision.

Pain is never enough

If your whole strategy for change is driven by your deep desire to get out of pain, soon enough that strategy will let you down.

Anthony Robbins describes this as the pressure cooker principle.[11] He says that one of the main reasons people don't change is they keep stepping in and out of the pressure cooker.

---

11   This concept comes from Anthony Robbins program *"The edge. The power to change your life now" https://www.tonyrobbins.com/pdfs/Workbook-The-Edge.pdf*

1. Pain leads to drive
2. Drive turns to action
3. Action improves results
4. Results lead to pleasure
5. Pleasure lessens the pain
6. Less pain leads to less drive
7. Less drive leads to less action
8. Less action eventually leads you back to where you started.

Pain avoidance is only ever half of the equation to produce lasting change. You'll need to be very clear about what you are moving away from, but also what you are desperate to move towards instead. Transformation requires pain *and* pleasure.

The second and equally important part of all motivation for change is being very clear about what you want to have happen for your life. Having a compelling vision for your life is the only thing strong enough to keep you marching forward in the face of great fear and seemingly insurmountable obstacles.

If you are waiting passively for your life to magically improve because you believe you somehow deserve it, you'll be waiting for the rest of your life while everyone else climbs all over the top of you. In the face of setbacks, misfortune, pain and disappointment there are only two questions powerful enough to get you out of bed in the morning to take your place in the race of life.

•   What do you really want?
•   What are you prepared to do about it?

The hero needs a quest

If you want to overcome insecurity, you've got to realise that it will be hard. The only way you will make it through the hard stuff is if you have a massive reason *why* you must find a way.

Stephen Covey says that the first habit of highly effective people is that they begin with the end in mind.[12] That is, they get very clear about exactly how they desire their life to be, and then they work their way backwards from there.

Without this compelling vision for your life driving you forward, you will simply give up when this journey gets too hard. If you don't have a driving mission, then what's the point of facing up to your fears and diving into the unknown? If Frodo isn't convinced that it is his personal mission to destroy the ring in the lake of fire, then I promise you he is not risking his life every day. He's going back home to bed!

The same will be true for you and me. Without a clear sense of what we truly want for our life, there is nothing to make sense of the risks and hardship involved in levelling up.

Developing your own vision

Sometimes the language of 'develop a compelling vision for your life' can feel a little intense and somewhat intimidating. It may seem that there is no room for error, and that this vision

---

12   Stephen R. Covey. *The 7 Habits of Highly Effective People,* Free press, New York, 1989

must magically appear before you in all its glory, in one profound moment in time, or else you are doing it wrong.

That is certainly not how it is for most people. Often the compelling life vision starts out as a blurry picture and you have to work it out from there. There is definitely some work to do for the vision to evolve and take shape.

Here's how I think about this idea of developing a compelling vision for my own life.

1. One of the ten relationship rules my wife and I have together is: Be clear about what you want to have happen. Holding each other to this standard means that complaining about what either of us don't want is never going to work. If I am unhappy about something in our marriage, or within the family unit, the question is always — so what do you want instead?

2. 'What do you want?' is the ultimate adult question. Of course I know what I want. It's just dangerous and difficult. This is the most beautiful, powerful and costly question I could entertain. However, all growth, innovation, discovery, and technological advancements have come as a direct result of adults having the courage to ask and answer that question. If I desire to fully be an adult, then this is the question on the table. The more I push into this question, the more it allows the best of me to emerge and for me to take my place in life. If it is the adult question, then it is my responsibility as an adult to push into this space and find

the answers. The world is waiting for me to take my place. This question is a beautiful gift and only good can come from me being courageous enough to answer it.

3. I practice journaling rituals with no accountability or judgment on this subject at least three times a week. I have fun with the exercise and allow myself to swing away. There is nothing I could write on my page that would be wrong or inappropriate. It is only when I notice patterns emerge on my 'What do I want' list that I pursue these desires more intently. When I've done all the hard work on exploring the highest intention behind the desire and all the consequences involved in pursuing the desire, then I'm able to set it as a well-formed outcome for my life.

4. I always go where the life is. This statement has become a major decision-making tool and always leads me deeper into the compelling vision for my life. Going where the life is always guides me toward resonance, and away from dissonance. When I don't know what to do, I go where the life is. When I'm not entirely sure about what I want, I will move towards the things that are life giving, and away from the things that seem to take life away.

5. Sometimes it works better to set intentions rather than goals. Roman emperor Marcus Aurelius famously said, "Our actions may be impeded...but there can be no impeding our intentions."

- Intentions are far less concerned with the details of how and when but are firmly focused on the end state instead. This allows much more flexibility with the vehicle or plan that is going to get me to where I want to be.
- I set intentions for all kinds of things: For my day, my meetings, my coaching sessions, for the books I am writing, my family holidays, dinner with friends, time with the kids, and date nights.
- Every time I set an intention I feel as though I'm experiencing the wonder of the ancient wisdom articulated so beautifully by the 13th century poet Rumi – 'What you seek is seeking you.' Setting intentions for every area of my life feels both powerful and graceful. It seems ambitious and relaxed. Like I am hopeful but not needy. It seems to me like I'm partnering with life itself.

Over the years, the power of setting intentions has given me the freedom to say yes and work out how later. All my favourite decisions in the key moments of my life have happened this way:

- Getting married
- Having kids
- Buying land
- Building houses
- Buying cars
- Becoming a pastor
- Becoming a high school chaplain
- Becoming a coach
- Starting my own business

- Starting a radio segment
- Moving to Germany
- Starting The Insecurity Project
- Starting a podcast
- Writing books
- Running international retreats

Life is not fair

Fully embracing practice four, means coming to terms with the simple fact that life is not fair. This is one of the most difficult but important life lessons I've ever had to work through. While this may seem to be a very pessimistic observation, it actually liberates and empowers us to succeed.

Getting what you want does not come because of what you deserve or how hard you work. Waiting and hoping that things will improve because you deserve it is a recipe for disaster. The moment you feel entitled, you risk incredible suffering. Just because you need something doesn't mean you'll get it. Just because you hope for something doesn't mean it will work out. Just because you try hard, doesn't mean you'll succeed. Just because you've earnt it, doesn't guarantee you'll be paid.

Bad things happen to good people every day. Evil people prosper, and good people go unrewarded all the time.

Life is not fair. The sooner you come to terms with this reality, the better it will be for you. Without this understanding many people see injustice as a valid reason to give up. Self-pity then takes over and life passes by.

Everyone gets given cards by virtue of the family they were born into. A simple survey of the state of global inequality highlights that there is nothing fair about this at all. The point is you've got to play the cards you've been dealt. Yes, things are not fair, but life responds to desire, commitment, creativity, resourcefulness, flexibility, resilience and inexorability. We each have the ability and responsibility to grow what we've been given and to improve our lot.

However, this only happens by knowing exactly what you want. Then you've got to be willing to adapt, grow and change to become the kind of person who has access to those kinds of results. Without giving up.

What do you want?

What are you prepared to do about it?

In the end, that is all that matters.

The only thing powerful enough to keep you moving forward in the face of adversity, injustice, setbacks, disappointments and failure is a compelling vision of how things MUST be for you.

The Insecurity Project

One of the biggest defining moments in the evolution of The Insecurity Project was when I first decided on the name. When I heard myself use that term for the first time, I knew it was right. It was a moment of clarity and certainty that resonated strongly.

I pitched it to my business coach the next day only for him to instantly tell me it was wrong. And that it breaks basic business rules. "You've got to pitch the prize not the problem. You should be called the security project, or the confidence guy, the self esteem coach. You need to let people know what you're going to get them, not focus on what's wrong with where they are now. The Insecurity Project is way too scary and confronting as the name of your business. People are insecure about being insecure. No one is putting their hand up to reveal how insecure they are let alone paying you money to help them fix it. So, what's your plan B when this doesn't work, Jaemin?"

I laughed it off and pretended not to be discouraged but went home with my tail between my legs and the wind taken out of my sails. Back to the drawing board. Two days later I was still in a funk about the conversation. I felt like it didn't matter that I liked the name, I wasn't allowed to use it. Someone whose opinion I respected had told me why it wouldn't work and so all I should do was find another name. The more I thought about it, the more disappointed and frustrated I got. It's not fair. Somehow a voice inside me snapped me out of my pity party.

Me: Stop being such a baby, Jaemin. He's not your mum. So what if he doesn't see your vision. Who cares if he doesn't think that name is right? It's not his name or his vision — it's yours! What do you want again?

Also me: With all my heart I want to lead a conversation globally about solving the insecurity problem. It makes the most sense to me to call this thing The Insecurity Project.

Me: And what are you prepared to do about it then?

Also me: All right! I'm in! All in! That is exactly what I'm going to do whether anyone else thinks it is a good idea or not.

Damn straight. That right there is where The Insecurity Project was born. The massive contribution my business coach gave me was the gift of resistance. When someone or something rises up and gets in your way, what are you going to do about it, cowboy?

The adult question

The 'what do you want?' question is what the child demands but is not ready for, and what the adult is ready for but doesn't trust themselves to answer.

As a parent, if you allowed your child to do whatever they wanted, they would ruin their life with that power. They do not have the maturity, self-awareness and emotional intelligence to deal with all that power. The loving parent creates boundaries, rules and structure for their children to obey so that they remain safe as they grow up. The child naturally resists the rules and pushes the boundaries because it is never fun being told what to do, yet this is how it must be.

However, by the time the child has become the adult and is finally ready to be the boss of their own life, all that power is super scary, and most people give it straight back! It turns out it is far safer and easier to let someone, or something, set the direction for your life. Then it is never your responsibility or your fault if things don't work out.

Yet to desire is human. Each of us know on some level what happiness and success would look like, we are just afraid that we don't have what it takes to get there. However, the moment we shut down true desire in our life in the interest of safety, we dehumanise ourselves and begin the process of atrophy and death.

Internal resistance

The interesting challenge with opening the desire box again, is that there is often massive internal resistance that shows up as confusion, lack of clarity and self-sabotage. All of this is driven from unresolved insecurity. The point is you don't have permission to entertain this question let alone go after what you want. It simply is not safe.

This marks another key milestone in the overcoming insecurity process. There are conditions for you to satisfy before you can proceed any further. The handbrake is on and the harder you try to force your way forward, the harder it stays on in return. You cannot win the battle against your own unconscious. It is far stronger than your conscious mind.

Before you feel paralysed at the thought of solving this new problem, the intention of all internal resistance is self-protection. And we only protect that which we value. In fact, the more value we place on something or someone, the more motivated we are to protect it. Therefore, all resistance is evidence of deep love. If we really didn't care about or like ourselves, it makes no sense to invest so much energy in being safe.

Think of your unconscious as the chief safety officer. The moment workplace health and safety rules are violated, everything gets shut down. If you want to get back to work and function at your best, it has got to be safe. Let me illustrate.

I enjoy running. It has been a central part of my life since I was 12. Over the Summer of 2018/19 I was particularly enjoying my running and felt fit and fast. In early February, it crossed my mind that I'd like to do Townsville marathon...again. The thought grew and I liked the sound of it so much that I informed my long-suffering wife that my plan was to sign up for another tilt at the title. The next day I woke up with debilitating sciatic pain. How frustrating!

Now when things are not kosher in my world, my internal angst gets stored in my piriformis muscle, which in turn grabs my sciatic nerve until I have solid pain from my bum down to my calf muscle in my left leg. I know my body well enough to understand that this is never the result of physical injury, but the quickest and surest way for my attention to be grabbed.

> *Jaemin there is a conversation to be had. We need to talk.*
>
> *When?*
>
> *Well now if you're ready.*
>
> *What if I'm not ready?*
>
> *I'll just keep this tension here in your left butt cheek and pull on your sciatic nerve, causing untold suffering and misery and putting the kybosh on all running until you are. No rush.*

A week later, I scheduled a meeting with myself. The first question I asked myself was why don't I have permission to run another marathon?

> *Wrong question...I'm not a jerk trying to ruin your life.*
>
> *Oh, sure, sorry. Better question. What would I need to do to get permission to run Townsville Marathon again this year?*

Now we are talking! Here's the thing J-man, when you pull the trigger on a marathon you go all in. It becomes an all-consuming thing for at least four months and everything else loses energy and focus. Now in the past that has been OK, but you've been working super hard on your business lately and as a result have seen some wonderful growth and progress. It would be super disappointing for you to take your eye off the goal and see things go backwards. I'm sure you'd agree that a marathon isn't worth jeopardising your business goals. Also, your family pay a significant price every time you start training for a marathon. You're tired, hungry, distracted, sore, and skinny so, it's not much fun for them. If you were capable of positioning marathon training as priority three, behind business and family, then it would be fine to go ahead with your plan.

(20 seconds of thinking time)

OK. I can abide with that. Great let's do it!

The next day I did a 14km run. And I had more sciatic pain than the day before. Bugger. Still no permission. With frustration I expressed to my subconscious that I agreed to the conditions and the pain was still there! What's up with that?

You didn't let me finish.

Oh, there's more? My apologies.

There's a second condition — every time you run Townsville Marathon you also get obsessed with winning the race. Your whole focus and language revolve around the fact that this is your year. It has to be. You visualise, memorise, idolise, exercise, metabolise all with the intention of bringing home the cash. Interestingly, on the previous five occasions, it hasn't been your year. You then suffer greatly due to immense disappointment of an unfulfilled dream. Even though every year you don't race, the winning time is slower than your PB, you can't control which super athlete show up on race day the year you fly north. Enough! I don't want to go through that disappointment again this time. It really is unnecessary. So, if you can genuinely take all ambitions of a podium finish off the table and run your own race, then it is ok to go ahead with your marathon plan.

So wait...can I still aim for a PB?

You can.

(35 seconds of more thinking time)

Ok. Yeah, look I can abide with those rules. I'm comfortable with that plan.

Going to sleep that night, I hear myself suggest that I should run 30kms in the morning. Weird. That kind of goes against gradually stepping up the training. I haven't run that far in 18 months. Ok sure.

I wake up before my alarm, run free and easy with zero pain. I get to the 20km mark though, and I'm done. I'm ready to head home. Yet, instead of turning right to end the run, my body takes me left. At every intersection I take the long way home until I arrive at my doorstep having run 30.2kms feeling strong and fast.

Incredible. Let's go run a marathon!

Finding internal resistance to achieving your big goals in life is very common. However, your ability to resolve this internal conflict will be a massive factor in the overall quality of your life and the level of success you achieve.

Rather than forcing your way forward through self-discipline and fighting against yourself to get the breakthrough, real resolution comes through awareness and understanding instead.

You are inherently good doing the best you know how. The way forward is not to force yourself to do that which you don't want to do, but to fully understand how this internal resistance is actually driven by love protecting you from what you fear. Deal with the fear and refocus the love and there is nothing that could stop you moving forward. Until you resolve all internal resistance to pursuing the desires of your heart, you will never fully press GO on chasing your big goals.

What is dangerous about success?

Another way of exploring the intention of this resistance is by understanding the sense of impending danger wrapped up in goals. I love that although this idea seems ridiculous at face value, if you sit with it a while, it always creates new awareness about the true nature of any internal resistance.

If you are finding it difficult to develop your compelling life vision, these are very powerful questions to ask yourself:

- What is dangerous about clarity?
- What is dangerous about confidence and certainty?
- What is dangerous about getting the things I say I really want?
- What is dangerous about being healthy, attractive, slim, well, rich and successful?

Although this may be hard to see, the truth is that if nothing were dangerous about the things you say you want, and there were no costs or risks involved, then you most certainly would have worked out how to achieve these goals already.

If you had total clarity about the vision for your life, you would no longer have any excuse for not stepping forward into this vision.

If you had all the confidence in the world, there would be

nothing stopping you putting yourself in the spotlight and speaking your message.

If you knew exactly what you wanted, then all the areas of your life which are different from this picture are instantly drawn into question. Additionally, you are now in conflict with everyone who wants something different for you or from you.

Success sets a standard that you now need to maintain. It changes the nature of how the people in your world relate to you. It brings attention, judgment, criticism and jealousy.

All of these things are incredibly dangerous because they instantly bring you closer to what you are afraid of and expose your deepest insecurities.

The point is that internal resistance to having a compelling vision highlights that there must be more pain associated to achieving the goal than in not achieving it. The safety officer has stepped in again and shut down production until conditions improve. Whether you want this to be true or not is entirely irrelevant. Your goals must be safe, or you will have to fight yourself to achieve them.

If your believable plan for success involves courage to overcome fear as your central driver that is not believable at all. Maybe in your 20's where you've got energy to waste and you're still running on the fuel of self-discipline, but then telling yourself to man up and just be more courageous, can't work in your 40's.

Your unconscious is not your enemy and you are not trying to ruin your own life. You are just deeply committed to not dying. Every cell in your body is hardwired for self-preservation. Good luck overriding that system without dehumanising yourself.

What would make this safe?

So now we've created some significant tension in the process. You are clear about what you want, but you realise you don't have permission to fully go after it until you've solved the insecurity problem.

In order to have the clarity, certainty and confidence you desire, it must also be safe. When I say safe, it only has to be safe enough. You are not looking for bubble wrap perfection, just a believable plan that feels solid.

The key safety question therefore becomes: What conditions would need to be satisfied until you had your own permission to move forward?

Without permission you are in trouble. Gaining permission to take the handbrake off will require you to become your own safety. Continuing to look for safety outside of you will no longer work. You can no longer convince yourself that the old plan of needing others to love, validate and accept you is going to keep you safe. That path hurts way too much. It only provides a sense of safety for a fleeting moment and then you feel unsafe again.

People let you down. They are too busy trying to get their own needs met without having the responsibility of meeting yours as well. Even when you do have great people in your world who are prepared to repeatedly encourage and support you, it means less and less to you because it feels like they have to do it and you question if they even really mean it.

The most dangerous way to position yourself in life is to contract your deepest emotional and psychological needs to your world. To need others to love, accept, agree, acknowledge, believe in, encourage, validate, and understand you in order to feel ok with yourself is fraught with danger. This strategy leaves you incredibly vulnerable and exposed to extreme risk.

Your world has immediate power to withhold the things you need to survive. Therefore, the only viable alternative is to be your own source of safety. True safety is to work out how to meet your own needs. How to love, accept, agree, acknowledge, believe in, encourage, validate, and understand yourself in order to feel OK. This means to be your own refuge. To be the one who deeply loves and accepts yourself means that you are now safe to explore anything in the world. If you've got your own back, what could possibly hurt you?

This is why solving the insecurity problem is so essential to a life well lived.

Practice 4 completes the other half of the motivation needed to solve this problem now.

The essence of practice 4 — Develop a compelling life vision:

The adult question — The most dangerous and powerful question we could ever ask ourselves is — What do you want? It is the question children crave but are not ready for, and the one adults are ready for, but become afraid of.

To desire is human — You do know what you want. It has just been shut down to play it safe. It is time to tap into the deepest desires of your heart again and develop a vision for your life that draws you forward.

Pleasure is the second part of all motivation — You need a 'moving away from' and 'moving towards' strategy to make change stick. More than just being clear about what you don't want, what do you want instead?

Why, not how — When the why becomes big enough the how takes care of itself. *How* is the slowest way to solve any problem. Be clear about why you must find a way to overcome insecurity.

You must have quest — A compelling vision for your life is the only thing powerful enough to sustain the journey when it gets hard. Begin with the end in mind. Lift your eyes to see why solving the insecurity problem is not just good for you, your family, or your business...It is good for the world.

Practice 5:
Get help from someone who doesn't care

Every hero needs a skilful guide. The key is to find one who doesn't get in the way and confuse everyone about who the hero is.

The fifth essential practice for overcoming insecurity is to get help from someone who has no vested interest in you achieving the goal and so simply serves your agenda.

The hero's guide

The thing about fear that makes it so powerful is that it feels so real. To an outsider it is clear that you are being irrational, but in your own head your thoughts and emotions are true, real and evidence backed. You are not making this stuff up! There is a monster about to consume you and you can feel the heat of its breath on your back as it draws ever closer.

Therefore, heroes need a skilful guide to prepare him or her for the journey ahead. In every hero's journey there is always the archetype of the wisdom character. There is always a Yoda, Gandalf, Dumbledore, Mr Miyagi, Teacher, Guru, Wizard, Coach, or Mentor. The wisdom character is essential to equip the hero, and then it is also essential that they know when to step back and let the hero do what only the hero can do.

Out of fear and into process

Fear and anxiety are often simply driven by our need for certainty. Stepping into process always gives us more resourceful forms of certainty, which displaces fear and anxiety. And because almost all debilitating fear is illogical, the way out of fear is into process.

Irrational fear feeds off uncertainty. It thrives in the space where you don't know what to do. Therefore, in every case, the way out of fear is into process. Trust the process. Rock climbing, business development, driving a car, buying a new house, getting married, learning to dance, starting a job at McDonalds — trust the process.

There is always a process that works. Find someone who has zero fear about the thing you are terrified about, and you'll notice that they have a well-worked process that they are completely confident in. If you allow them to take you through the process they use, you'll come out the other side completely fine. To have someone with the ability to take you out of story and into process is an essential part of the process of eradicating any fear.

Objectivity

True objectivity is practically impossible for a human being. We are sense-making creatures always telling stories about our experience of life. Our brain is constantly filtering a sea of possibilities to only find evidence for whatever we believe is relevant, important or true. Everything else MUST be deleted or distorted or else we would be in complete information over-load trying to objectively assess what each individual piece of information really means. For this reason, solving the insecurity problem on your own is incredibly unlikely. In order to change the story you are living out of, you need to get outside it. That requires objectivity.

One of the reasons I love the coaching space so much is that it offers the cleanest and most objective conversation of any relational frame. True coaching is simply about getting a person more of what they really want. It is a role with no agenda other than to serve. The coach has no vested interest in the outcome of the client, which makes it a truly judgment free space.

Because insecurity exists as a story in our own head, and because our heads are evidence-gathering machines, these stories become our truth. We have years of hard evidence to support our beliefs that our deep fears are likely to be true. This level of subjective experience is a massive part of the problem and so to solve it, a very high level of objectivity is required. To have someone with the ability to take you out of story into process and help you gain some high-level perspective about the truth of your existence is an essential part of the process. The key distinction here is that it cannot be someone who has a vested interest in seeing you sort out your stuff. It is impossible to help others change without creating a truly judgment free space. Wanting them to change is the least useful you could possibly be.

Insights, opinions and advice

Intuition is one of the great human qualities. The ability to understand something instinctively, without the need for conscious reasoning gives each of us the capacity to access a profound realm of truth. This truth when revealed by another human being can cut to the core of our reality and expose things hidden to our normal sense-making paradigms.

Having a keen sense of intuition for what is happening in another person's life is a powerful gift, however, there are a few major challenges with this gift of seeing clearly:

1. Just because you can see it does not mean you also have permission to say it.
2. If you speak into another person's reality without their permission it doesn't matter how right you are, you will be wrong.
3. The quickest way to break rapport and trust with another person is to judge them. You no longer are a safe person and therefore there is a natural guardedness and closed positioning to all you might have to say to them in the future.

4.   No one's intuition is perfect. Whatever you can see is still coloured by your own cognitive biases.

Therefore, the real skill of intuition is developing your capacity to deal appropriately with what you can see. Intuition and truth telling are without doubt among the most dangerous tools humans possess. To use them carelessly is to play with fire. While there is so much potential for good, often the intuition is ruined by the delivery and therefore creates unimaginable relationship chaos.

Consider this severe warning about the power of the words we speak to others from the bible.

James 3:1-7

1.   My brothers and sisters, not many of you should become teachers, because you know that we who teach will be judged more strictly.
2.   We all make many mistakes. If people never said anything wrong, they would be perfect and able to control their entire selves, too.
3.   When we put bits into the mouths of horses to make them obey us, we can control their whole bodies.
4.   Also a ship is very big, and it is pushed by strong winds. But a very small rudder controls that big ship, making it go wherever the pilot wants.
5.   It is the same with the tongue. It is a small part of the body,

but it brags about great things. A big forest fire can be started with only a little flame.

6. And the tongue is like a fire. It is a whole world of evil among the parts of our bodies. The tongue spreads its evil through the whole body. The tongue is set on fire by hell, and it starts a fire that influences all of life.

For someone to actually be useful to you, you definitely need them to say what they see. However, it is only those who have refined their capacity to NOT speak into your reality until they have permission to do so, that gains the right to share their insights.

In his best-selling book, *The Coaching Habit,*[13] Michael Bungay Stanier pleads with coaches to drop the judgment and lead with curiosity. To cultivate this, habit two of seven in his model is simply to respond to the information given with the question "What else?" When a coach holds the space with this simple question, it always leads to more awareness for the client. This proves to be an essential part of the transformation process, because it empowers the person to discover their own results.

"If you could just stay curious a little longer and not be in such a hurry to move to advice and action that would make such a difference to the quality of the conversations."
MICHAEL BUNGAY STANIER

---

13   Michael Bungay Stanier, *The coaching habit, Say less, ask more and change the way you lead forever,* Box of Crayons Press, Toronto 2016

The subject object switch

Harvard Psychologist Robert Keegan[14] believes that the sub-ject- object shift is the single most important move we can make to accelerate personal growth. Being subjective about our experience is a natural and wonderful part of being human. Our experiences are precisely that – ours! The issue is that while ever we are inside these experiences, we have no ability to change them. It is only as we step outside of our own filters, perception and cognitive biases and gain distance from our subject experience that we gain the ability to adjust the lens.

This ability to be self-aware and to think about our thinking is perhaps what most distinctly differentiates us from animals. Every moment spent being objective about the choices we are making always gives us more awareness and more choice. When we have more choice, we naturally make better choices. It is the illusion of no choice characterised by being in the subject space that leaves us feeling stuck.

Increased awareness

Therefore, the role of the coach/wisdom character/guide is to help you see what you cannot see by helping you gain some distance between you and your story. The power of this added awareness is that it always brings more choice. This is another essential part of the process in overcoming insecurity for good. In order to set yourself free, you must get out of your own head.

14   Steven Kotler and Jamie Wheal, *Stealing Fire,* Harper Collins New York, 2017 P.38

Accountability

Contrary to popular opinion, the role of the coach/wisdom character/guide is not to provide accountability. Accountability, like self-discipline, is massively overrated. I see lots of people looking for someone to hold them accountable in the areas their own self-discipline is letting them down. Self-discipline is supposed to let you down remember. That is not so some-one else can pick up the slack for you, but so you can source your own deep internal motivation in the form of self-permis-sion instead.

Accountability gives a false sense of progress. If you are only making changes because of the pain of having someone else kick your arse if you don't, then the moment the threat of that pain stops, and they stop holding you accountable, all motiva-tion for change stops too.

If you need someone else to make you do the stuff you don't want to do, then the take home point is, you don't actually want to do it. All lasting change is driven from a place of being clear about what it is that you want and taking responsibility to do whatever it takes to achieve it — because you want it. If you don't want it, no amount of someone else wanting it for you is going to change your results.

Unhelpful words

Language is far more powerful than most people imagine. The words we use don't just describe our experience; they shape it.

Changing your words will change your experience. One of the most useful roles of the coach/wisdom character/guide is to mirror back the exact language patterns you are using to see the impact these words are having on your experience of life.

Self-deception

The great American physicist Richard Feynman says, "The first principle is that you must not fool yourself — and you are the easiest person to fool**."**

One of the ways this plays out most frequently in the change journey is empty promises and false commitment to improvement. Using language that feels so full of intention and commitment, but in reality, is vacuous and evasive. The intention of this language is to trick you and others into assuming you're all in, when all you really want is an out.

A magician's only real trick is the art of drawing attention to one thing to hide it from another. This kind of language is a classic example of misdirection:

Need to...

This is language of judgement. The intention of all self-judgment is to protect ourselves from the judgment of others. If I tell myself I need to do it, then you don't need to tell me as well. It sounds as though you've committed to something, so we can stop talking about it. However, if you were to review the data around how often you say you *need* to do something against how often you actually do that thing, you'd find it is more likely to get in the way of action than providing any kind of motivation or intention.

> *How are you going with that coaching exercise on secondary gain?*

> *Look I really need to get onto that. I need to stop putting it off. I've just been so busy.*

> *I need to set aside some time to focus on it this weekend.*

The truth is you don't *need* to do anything, especially in the judgment-free space. This is another great example of the value of being precise in your speech.

Do you want to do it? If not, what's the resistance telling you?

Are you going to do it? If not, be clear about that. Own your decision. There is no right or wrong.

Try to...

Yoda's famous wisdom on the subject of trying is "Do or do not do, there is no try." Basically, when you say you're going to try, you're actually saying I'm not going to do anything.

The intention of this misdirection is to give you an out. I tried, but it didn't happen so it's not my fault.

Where are you up to with that conversation you were going to have with your dad?

I've been trying to talk to him, but he always turns the conversation back away from the issues I'm trying to address. I'm really going to try and make some time to tell him how I feel this week.

Being dishonest takes power away from yourself. Using the language of 'try to' sounds like you are committing to the necessary action, but the honesty of the situation is that you are afraid, unwilling or uncertain and this language is part of your protection strategy to avoid pain. While the intention of 'trying to' do things is always about safety, trying turns out to be hazardous to your long-term health and happiness. It leaves you in the dangerous middle ground of indecision.

Over the years of watching my son at the local skate park I've seen more than my fair share of carnage. Watching kids learning to drop into the half pipe is particularly amusing, disturbing and also educational. As a general rule, the kids who get hurt the most are those who *try* and drop in. You can smell their half-hearted reluctance from the car park. Nevertheless, as they give it a go, their balance and weight distribution reflect their general concern for life and limb and therefore tend to be on the back foot which sends the board shooting from beneath them. The only way to drop into a half pipe is to drop into the half pipe. You either drop in or you don't. Half dropping in gets you a concussion.

Likewise, you can't try to have an important conversation with someone. You can't try to lose weight or gain fitness. And you certainly can't try to face your fear and overcome insecurity. You either do it or don't do it. Yes or no. In or out. Committed or uncommitted.

Hope to...

Often this language pattern demonstrates false hope. False hope is wishing things would get better but believing deep in your heart that they won't ever improve. It's feeling that you deserve more but knowing you're stuck with your lot in life.

How are you feeling about your future?

Fingers crossed; I really hope things start to improve in my life. I'm hoping this course will work for me.

Real hope on the other hand is simply a product of embracing 100% choice. The moment you live with the illusion of no choice and succumb to the victim mindset, hope evaporates because you are out of options to improve your situation. You have no control and the belief that you have no real choice in the matter.

Wanting, wishing, hoping, longing, all while managing a residual disappointment is the experience of false hope. If you remain in this space for too long, it gets inside you and inevitably dials down your expectation of life.

The point of my story is this. Don't confuse yourself by thinking all hope is the same. The only way to live with genuine hope is to position yourself with 100% choice. Sure, you don't always get to choose what happens to you, but you do get to choose your response. The moment you embrace choice, it is impossible to ever feel hopeless!

I Can't...

This is perhaps the laziest attempt of misdirection. It's a straight up lie that screams amateur hour. What you mean when you say I can't is – I don't want to. Which is totally fine by the way. We disempower ourselves with anything other than the truth of our situation.

> I've tried everything and I can't lose weight. I can't connect with my kids. I can't confront my partner. I can't work out what this is about. I can't get clear about what I want. I've done everything I can, so now it is out of my hands.

If you don't find a way out of these disempowering language patterns, it will be impossible to solve the insecurity problem. It is incredibly difficult to observe your own language patterns while being inside them.

Obviously, you need help to overcome your insecurity, but getting help is full of danger at the same time. Often the biggest threat to the hero being the hero is the guide themselves. There are many rescuers disguising themselves as guides. That is, people who like to fix others, give advice and like to be the one who is needed and depended on. The biggest challenge for coaches, counsellors, and psychologists is not to get in the way and confuse everyone about who the hero is.

The Karpman drama triangle

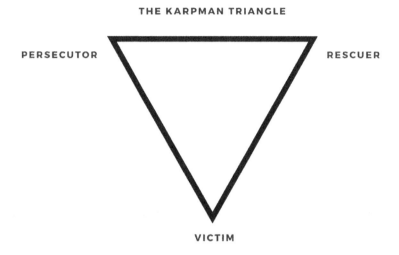

THE KARPMAN TRIANGLE

PERSECUTOR

RESCUER

VICTIM

The Karpman drama triangle[15] explains the danger of the victim and rescuer roles perfectly. Here is how it works:

The Victim:

The Victim's position is "Poor me!" They feel oppressed, hopeless, powerless, and seem unable to make decisions or solve their own problems. They complain about how unfair and unjust the world is and constantly look to blame someone or something for their difficulties.

---

15   The drama triangle was conceived by Stephen Karpman, a student studying under Eric Berne, the father of transactional analysis in 1968.

In order to stay within the relative safety of this well-developed role, the Victim, if not being persecuted, will seek out a Persecutor and also a Rescuer who will save the day but also perpetuate the Victim's negative feelings.

The Rescuer:

The rescuer's overt position is always to help victims. However, while it appears that they are motivated by justice, compassion or service, they actually become an enabler to the victim. Their rescuing has negative effects: It keeps the Victim dependent and gives the Victim permission to fail, perpetuating the dysfunctional cycle. The rescuer feeds off the role they get to play. The rescuer needs the victim just as much as the victim needs the rescuer.

Ultimately, the rescuer finds their identity in being the person called upon to save the day. The moral superiority they gain by righting the wrongs caused by the persecutor helps add to their sense of significance. They enjoy having someone depend on them and draw value from being seen to go the extra mile to appear to help those in need. Additionally, by focusing their energy on fixing someone else's dysfunctional situation, the attention is drawn away from any dysfunction in their own life. Their own problems are disguised as concern for the victim's needs.

The Persecutor:

The persecutor plays the role of the bully. They throw fuel on the fire by finding someone to oppress. They are often controlling, critical, angry, authoritarian, rigid, and superior. They exploit the weakness of the victim for their own gain and elevate their status in life by holding power over those under them. The persecutor is the villain in the story and gives energy to the victim by giving them someone to blame.

Author David Emerald introduced a beautiful way out of the drama triangle, suggesting that the victim is the only one who can break the triangle. They do so when they adopt the alternative role of creator, view the persecutor as a challenger, and enlist a coach instead of a rescuer.[16]

As the victim begins to see themselves as the creator, they start looking for their own solutions and are outcome focussed rather than dwelling on the problems. When the victim sees the persecutor as the challenger instead, they become aware of the gift for growth this person offers. As the victim rises to the challenge and stands up to the bully, often the cycle of victimhood is broken for good.

Finally, Emerald says that rather than looking for someone to rescue them, the victim should seek out a coach who has the capacity to empower them to solve their own problems.

Objective embodied wisdom

The kind of person who will be most useful to you will demonstrate these three characteristics:

• They can maintain distance as a dispassionate observer

---

16   David Emerald. *The power of TED (The empowerment dynamic),* Polaris publishing, 2015

without imposing their map of the world onto yours. As such they do not bring their own desired outcomes for you into the conversation but hold the space for you to form your own.

- They have real world wisdom to share out of the abundance of their own experience.
- They fully embody their message. There is clear evidence of them having their own hero's journey that they have given themselves to entirely. Interestingly, the only way to be an effective life coach is to smoke what you are selling. Your ability to be useful to others comes out of the overflow of your own personal development journey.

The key distinction here is that it cannot be someone who has a vested interest in seeing you sort out your stuff. Could you imagine if Mr Miyagi dealt with the bullies for Daniel-son so he never had to face them? And what if Gandalf told Frodo to give him the ring and then magically made it disappear so that everyone could go back to their ordinary life?

I promise you if that were the case, no one is watching these movies. That would be a boring story. The same is true in your life, people can rescue you from your challenges rather than empower you to become the person who can solve the problem yourself.

Practice 5 proves that in order to solve the insecurity problem in your life, it is essential to get help. The important distinction, however, is to get the right help at the right time.

The essence of practice 5 – Get help from someone who doesn't care:

The hero needs a guide – In order to solve the insecurity problem, you need embodied wisdom from someone who has already navigated this path effectively in their own life.

Caring is useless — Wanting and caring is natural from friends and family, but it is the least useful tool for helping people change. You need to find someone who is not trying to rescue you and has no agenda other than to serve. This means they won't get in the way.

Objectivity is essential – The subject object switch accelerates human growth more than any other thing. In order to change your story, you'll have to get some distance from it first. The role of the guide is to get you out of your story and into process.

You are the hero in this story – No one is coming to save you. The guide needs to hold a judgment-free space and position you as a responsible adult who has already created the current results, and therefore, is entirely capable of creating different results.

Practice 6:
Be the hero

No one is coming to save you. You created this mess, and you are the only one who can clean it up.

The sixth essential practice for overcoming insecurity is to do what only the hero can do and go slay the dragon.

Face the fear

In Joseph Campbell's defining work, *The Hero with A Thousand Faces*, he shows that in all the stories we love, at some point the hero steps up and does what only the hero can do. It is a wonderful metaphor that parallels each of our journeys as the hero in our own story.

"It is only when a man tames his own demons that he becomes the king of himself if not of the world."
JOSEPH CAMPBELL

When it comes to overcoming insecurity, no one can do it for you. You are the one that created this monster, and you are the only one with the power to destroy it. There is work to be done, fear to be faced and dragons to be slayed. And YOU are the hero who is going to get it all done. All previous five stages are preparation for stage six. It's crunch time.

When it comes to fear, our natural instinct is to run away from the thing we are afraid of, yet the hero is the one who shows up with incredible courage and marches straight into battle instead. In order to overcome insecurity in your life, at some point you've got to go explore the things you are most afraid of about yourself to see how true they really are. Is there any substance to this fear of not being good enough? There is only one way to find out for sure, and it involves going to the heart of what you are MOST afraid of.

The incredible thing is that everyone else can see that you will actually be OK. The monster in the cave you fear is actually not a monster at all, just a couple of mice playing silly buggers with a candle and some tin cans projecting a huge shadow and making a big noise.

Just like The Wizard of Oz, it is all smoke and mirrors. But until you actually go and face it you will never know for sure. Everyone else knows you have always been enough and always will be, but you've got to go work that out for yourself.

The monster only exists in your head. It appears to be real, concrete and external. Although you've always been convinced that surely everyone can see that you're not good enough, the truth is everyone thinks you're fine. They are too busy fighting their own monsters to worry about yours anyway. The only way of finding out if this is true is to front up and face the monster. You either die or come out the other side reborn.

Dealing with shame

To make matters worse, most of the things we fear about ourselves are wrapped in a layer of shame. Therefore, you have to deal with the shame before you can work on the fear. The underlying fear that drives shame is that if you really knew me, and what I've done, you'd reject me. Therefore, there is only one way to really overcome shame. You have to face your own behaviour and understand why you did it.

Is it because you are bad?

Is it because you are wrong?

Is it because you are not enough?

Now while it is typical to judge ourselves, and others by what we do, the truth is we are not our behaviour. In fact, every behaviour (even the most negative behaviour) has a positive intention. We are simply trying to bring peace and comfort to ourselves. All behaviour is an attempt to meet our core needs of certainty, variety, significance, love, contribution and growth. We don't do bad things because we are bad; we do bad things because we are needy.

Now this doesn't justify the behaviour, but it also doesn't change the fact that we are inherently good, trying to do the best we know how. The only way out of shame is to face yourself in the mirror and still be able to deeply love and accept yourself. I know exactly what I've done and why I've done it, and I still like me. Now there is nothing to prove or defend.

Reconcile the past

Most people's strategy for dealing with the mess and pain of their past is to distance themselves from these experiences by all means possible. The problem is that wherever you go, there you are. Past issues that remain unresolved linger as a residual loss on the balance sheet of your life. They weaken and undermine your net worth, or more specifically, your self worth. Deep down you fear these things reveal something terrible about you. Therefore, there could be no benefit in exploring them. Supress, mask, medicate, avoid and hope they just go away.

The thing is they never go away. You know this to be true. It is the work of the hero to stop running from the past and to turn and face it instead. Until you fully reconcile the events and experiences of the past, you cannot move forward, unhindered, into your future. Remember, you have given meaning to EVERY experience in your past. Whether you are aware of it or not, you have done so by the way you've answered the two central sense making questions; Why did this happen?; and what does it mean about me?

If you do not have a genuinely positive and empowered answer to these questions that you've fully bought into, the only other option is that you've decided bad things are true about you instead. Being the hero means it is time to go back and review the data around what went down and what you made it mean.

Death and rebirth

One of the most painful and most important themes of the hero's journey is that of death and rebirth. This motif is a central part of mythology, religion and nature. We see it most clearly in the example of the butterfly. The caterpillar comes to the end of that way of being, is wrapped in a cocoon, forms into a chrysalis and then emerges reborn into a butterfly. It is this coming to the end of oneself and not clinging to the old form but rather surrendering to the emergence of something new that captures the deep transformation of the hero. Death makes way for new birth. That is the cycle of life.

There comes a point in a person's life in facing up to their deepest fears about themselves that they realise they've come too far to turn back to the ordinary world. They will either face the monster and die or emerge out the other side reborn.

When the hero returns, they are not the same person. A deep transformation has taken place to reveal a new and beautiful version. In order for this to truly take place, part of them must die. There is no other way.

No one is coming to save you

Sooner or later, in every hero's journey narrative, the wisdom character fades into the background or disappears altogether. The monster still needs defeating and only the hero remains. It is often a dreadful moment of discovery to realise that no one is coming to save you and that you are actually the hero in this story.

If someone else could have solved your insecurity problem for you by now, they would have.

Have you ever noticed how painfully vacuous other people's comments about your wonderfulness really are? Well-meaning rescuers fill social media with this ineffective content daily.

Imagine if all you needed to do was read a misquoted statement from the Dali Lama with a sunrise background telling you to stop worrying about what others think of you and just realise you are enough! We'd all feel great about ourselves and could throw books like this one in the bin.

That is obviously not how this works. Insecurity gives you a real-world, high-stakes, life and death, opportunity for self-discovery. The fact that you have every opportunity to go home, give up, give in, fail, fall, die, or regress means the drama of your life is compelling viewing for your world. Everyone is holding their breath to see what will happen next.

Discover the origin

In order to overcome insecurity, it is essential to go backwards before you can really move forward again. To untangle the messy stories of lack, limitation and insecurity, can only be done effectively by tracing the root of the story all the way back to when it was first created.

Most people try and deal with the mess in their heads by pretending it doesn't exist or through self-medication and various other coping strategies. It often feels too painful and overwhelming to try and untangle the mess and get to the bottom of it. Yet, without going back to where that limiting story was first created means you are always managing mess inside your head and heart that is stopping you being at your best. Any attempt to write new stories and develop new beliefs is undermined by the fact that subconsciously you still believe your original story is true.

It is like trying to build a new house on a crumbling old foundation. When it comes to lasting transformation, we each must come to terms with the fact that all we have is story and then become absolutely aware of exactly what our story is. A great way to do this is simply to observe your patterns of behaviour. Behaviour never lies. It always flows out of our beliefs. Ask yourself; *what must I believe in order to behave this way?*

You can imagine why some of your current results are less than ideal if you are in fact still living out of scripts written by a 4-year-old! Once you are clear about the nature and patterns of your own story, then it must be possible to trace this story all the way back to the beginning. When was the first time you told yourself this was true? Who else had a part in writing this story with you?

Often people tell me that they simply can't remember or have no idea where the story started. They wonder if it is even possible to become aware of the origin especially if the beginning of the story was very early in life. Yet this vital information can always be discovered if and when you are ready.

Our conscious mind has limited storage capacity. It's a bit like a small flash drive. There is enough room for some pictures and videos and a few songs, but not much more. However, our subconscious mind is like unlimited cloud-based storage. Every single thing we have ever seen, heard or experienced is all stored there somewhere. Of course, defining moments such as the origin of the single most destructive story in your life has been recorded and a file has been created. The issue is you have to get clearance to view it.

As part of your internal self-protection strategies, your subconscious is keeping that information from you until you are ready to deal with it. Otherwise, it may only cause you more pain. The implications of the discovery of the origin of your story is that there must also be a time in your life BEOFRE this story was true for you. This means, the story you are living out of is not you. It is an addition to your life; it is not who you are. It is an imposition to the real you. You have picked up this story and worn it like a jumper. You have then identified with this jumper and it has become how you've seen yourself and how others have seen you. However, it is just a jumper, and you could take it off and appear very differently.

When you discover and change the first time, the whole house of cards built on this foundation comes down as well.

Deconstruct the story

The central part of practice six is to fully deconstruct limiting stories all the way back to where they first started. Underneath every issue in our lives is some kind of limiting belief about our own value and worth. The research suggests these beliefs almost always originate in our lives before we are seven. Therefore, a large part of the work of the hero is to go back and explore the stories they told about themselves when they were a child.

I'm sure you've heard it said that you can't change the past. But what if that was not entirely true? At this stage in the process there is generally a fair bit of trepidation in going back into the pain and trauma of the past. In fact, this is why many people avoid the change process altogether! Why would anyone want to go digging around in the past? What good could possibly come from it?

Yet here's the secret. You don't have to go digging into the things that happened to you, just into what you made those things mean. You are simply reviewing the story telling data. You are examining the opinions you formed in these moments based on the limited data you were working with at the time. What if you now have access to new and updated data?

Review the data

When I was a kid, I was convinced Tooheys Draught was pro-nounced 'tootheys drort' and that 400m circular cycling tracks were called a melodome. I was gutted when I found out neither was accurate. As soon as I had been given more data, my old data was obsolete. I didn't have to force myself to change the story; it just stopped making any sense.

I know you feel that all your current data is accurate, but the moment you discover that there are gaps and holes all through it; you couldn't hang onto the old story even if you wanted to. You are not stupid. If you know something doesn't make sense, then it doesn't make sense! If it's just a data review exercise, you'll probably be ok too. It may not be anywhere near as scary as you've always imagined.

The point is, life is not based on the things that happen to us, but on the meaning we place on those events, conversations and experiences. Therefore, if you change the meaning, you change your experience. Which also means the past becomes very different.

Practice 6 is crunch time. To be the hero in your own story, and to justify that title, certainly means there is some significant work to do. All roads are leading straight towards the thing you've always been most afraid of. The only sure way to find out if you are enough is to go face the monster.

The essence of practice 6 – Be the hero:

Face the monster – At some stage you will need to face insecurity head on. Are you good enough or not? The only way out is through.

Discover the origin — There is always an origin or inception point to limiting beliefs. It is crucial to deconstruct the limiting beliefs and fear all the way back to where they started.

Reconcile the past — Until you fully reconcile past choices, bad mistakes and poor behaviour, they linger as a residual loss on your personal balance sheet and weaken your confidence for the future.

Review the data – Go back and explore the defining moments of your past, and specifically, what you made them mean about you. New data makes old data obsolete.

Deconstruct the old story — Until you break down the old story, and until it doesn't make sense anymore, it will always be the prevailing narrative if your life.

Practice 7:
Re-write the story

You are not the actor in the story. You are the story-teller. You wrote the first version, so you know how to write the new one too.

The seventh essential practice for overcoming insecurity is to re-write the story. This final stage in the process makes sure the changes you have created in the previous six stages really stick.

It's your story

While discovering the origin of your insecurity story is crucial, in order to really set yourself free, the process needs to go to the next stage. Take responsibility for the fact that you are not just an actor in the story, but you are the storyteller. If you don't like the stories you have told about your life to this point, you and only you, can go back and write new ones.

This process it not easy, but neither is it complicated. We are sense-making creatures who go into the world and tell stories to give meaning to our experiences. It's all just a story though. It's all a work of fiction. There are a multitude of other stories that could be told about the same experience. Each story leads to a very different destination.

The crucial part of this stage is that you take full ownership of the stories you tell about your own value and worth. It all comes down to what you believe about yourself. Ultimately insecurity is overcome when you decide that you are enough. All along, it's only ever been your opinion that has held any weight. Now is your chance to create an opinion that allows you to go free.

Deep Change

For so many people, the idea that things could actually get better occupies the same mental hard drive as fairy tales and magic potions. It is not the real world. For that reason, they have given up hope and are left to fantasise about things they know will never take place. However, when you grasp the science of how transformation happens, lasting change moves from being a fairy tale for super-humans, to something natural and normal. Imagine how relaxed you'd feel about the quality of your life naturally improving if you aligned yourself with the things that made it inevitable and even unavoidable!

I absolutely love what becomes possible when troubling human behaviour is tackled with a system-thinking approach. It helps turn what appears to be messy, mysterious and unknowably weird things into strategic, clear, cause and effect operations. People work perfectly. The results we get are the exact results we've designed our system to produce. They are not broken, random or weird. This then allows the process of self-aware-ness to become all about reviewing scientific data.

Remember, if our behaviour is a system, then there is a design. If there is a design, then there is a strategy. If there is a strategy, there is an intention. If there is an intention it can be observed. If it can be observed, it can be deconstructed. If it can be deconstructed it can be changed and if it can be changed than it can be improved and reconstructed!

Operating system upgrade

One of my favourite metaphors for this work therefore is that deep change is simply the process of upgrading your operat-ing system. Imagine trying to install apps developed in 2020 with the original iOS for the iPhone 3! The old system has no capacity to run the modern app. It is completely incompatible. Similarly, I frequently see people trying to handle the complexi-ties of adult life with the operating system they developed as a child or a teenager — no wonder things are not going well for them. The cool thing is that you developed and installed the original operating system so you are already proficient in systems technology. You know how to do this.

A client of mine was looking to find more confidence to write and speak his message to the world. His intention was to become more assertive and committed at showing up and putting himself out there. In spite of all his intention, however, there was massive internal resistance to this idea that kept him from this plan.

When we turned the lights on and had a look under the surface, we discovered that his operating system had no inbuilt capacity for conflict. So the moment someone disagreed or was mildly offended at his viewpoint, it created massive anxiety and withdrawal.

It turns out that after a period of teenage rebellion that caused significant stress and pain to his parents, he developed a strategy to win back their love. If he was agreeable, responsible and always did what was right, then they could trust him again. He was insecure that this period of rebellion revealed something deeply flawed about his character so his plan for feeling like a good person was to be liked and respected. In this system, assertiveness and independence would only lead to conflict. Conflict was dangerous because it could remove all the things he needed to feel like a good human being. And you can't run assertiveness apps in an operating system that has deleted any space for conflict.

In addition to this, he also discovered that the word unhindered was deeply troubling and created significant anxiety. The last time he was unhindered, he was reckless. It was definitely not safe to take the handbrake off for fear of what would happen. His current operating system was defined by self-discipline and playing by other people's rules.

What conditions need to be satisfied to have permission to take the handbrake off? He had to build a new operating system capable of knowing how to deliver great results and handle the complexity of living a meaningful life on his own terms. The final piece in his change journey as he re-wrote the story was therefore to build a new operating system.

There are five aspects of the whole system upgrade. These five things will help you draw all the content and frameworks of this book together into a concise and believable plan to see you truly be unhindered by self doubt, irrational fear and insecurity.

The upgraded operating system produces completely different results than the original system. Change, growth and improvement is all that could possibly happen. As you upgrade the system, transformation becomes entirely inevitable. You couldn't not experience better, more desirable results in every area of your life!

Upgrade 1: Child to Adult

The first part of the system upgrade is to move from operating as a child to operating as an adult. One of the simplest ways to understand genuine personal development is that it is simply the journey of fully becoming an adult. It is the role of parents to prepare their children for adulthood and while most people get this means being physically and financially self-sufficient, the idea of emotional, relational and intellectual maturity is often completely overlooked. This leaves many people growing up physically, while remaining childlike, dependent and needy in many other areas.

The key is to be the adult in your own life. That is hard, but important. There is no way around it. This means:

- Taking full responsibility for your response to life rather than being a victim of what others say and do to you.
- Meeting your needs for love, significance and certainty internally rather than externally (being fully self-sufficient).
- Being clear about what you want and taking full responsibility to make it happen.

While this is hard work, the great news is that every cell in your body is designed for adulthood. It is the natural order of things, and it is only doubt, fear and insecurity that leave us clinging to childish ways.

One of the core components of adulthood is self-sufficiency. That means to be able to fill your own cup. Most adults are able to meet their own needs physically and financially, but are still dependent on others relationally, emotionally, psychologically and intellectually. This dependence means they defer to others wisdom, wait for other people to solve their problems and look for others to validate them.

There is still a lot of strange rhetoric about the idea that being a child is somehow easier than being an adult; *Don't grow up — it's a trap! This adult stuff is hard!* Yet to imagine that your childhood was completely carefree and that your core needs were met perfectly at all times is to view the past with rose coloured glasses. This view cannot be sustained under any kind of scrutiny. It is simply not true.

For so many people being a kid was extremely hard. Trying to navigate increasing complexity with minimal awareness, maturity and emotional intelligence is a nightmare! Add to this the challenge of finding a way to feel loved and important from those around you, and you've got a recipe for some serious suffering.

Surely growing up must make things easier. Well, only if you upgrade the operating system. If you have only grown up physically and financially but are still running all the child software for love, certainty and significance, you're in for some pain.

Upgrading from meeting your needs as a child externally to fully becoming the adult capable of meeting your needs internally is the essence of the personal development journey. Change is inevitable when you fully become an adult and upgrade the quality of your life by *being* an adult in every area of your life.

The chief validator

One of the most important things in life is to feel a sense of significance and that you matter in the world. When we were young it was very natural to look to our parents to give us this sense of value. Whether you are aware of assigning this role or not, at some point you made them the ones with the power to say whether or not you mattered. Therefore, much was done to gain their approval so you could feel worthwhile.

Some parents are better than others at giving, but while ever you have an external source of self-worth, it is never lasting. You never fully believe it and even if you do get what you're looking for it lasts for such a short time before you are craving it again.

No matter who we are or what our story is, at some point we must all find a way to take the power back and work out how to tell ourselves that we are enough rather than depending on that from others. This means firing your parents (or anyone else for that matter) from the role of validator in your life and reassigning that role to yourself. It's time to validate yourself. This upgrade involves cutting off all the external outsourcing and bringing operations back in-house. This means:

- Filling your own cup
- Trusting your own judgement
- Referencing your own wisdom
- Validating your own existence
- Becoming your own refuge

Upgrade 2: Treating symptoms to Dealing with the core

This upgrade is to fully buy into the awareness that people work perfectly. You are not broken. Your results are the exact results you've designed your system to produce. This allows you to avoid the trap of behaviour managing yourself by treating the symptoms.

Change strategy 1.0 typically revolves around solving problems in the exact place the pain shows up. It is a simple level of cause and effect that certainly delivers a measure of short-term change. If I have pain in my health, then it must be a health problem. Relationship pain proves there is a relationship problem. Trouble with money, then clearly it is a money problem.

This operating system works for a season because of the scope we have for inefficiency and optimism. The fact that nothing is actually changing or improving doesn't really dampen our hope for the future as long as we keep telling ourselves we are getting there.

I used to meet weekly for support and accountability with a local colleague. Each week when I asked how he was going his unwavering response every time was "we are getting there."

I always used to think, really? Are you actually? Getting where exactly? It seemed to me that things are exactly the same as every other time. His response eventually wore me down until I could bear it no more. Thankfully, the gift of pain, along with the law of diminishing returns, gives us all an opportunity to see the folly of continually adjusting the end product rather than changing the settings in the factory.

Behaviour management is exhausting. That is all it can be. It is nothing more than a futile effort to stem the tide of what is produced effortlessly and continuously by your current operating system. It feels like nothing is changing because nothing *is* changing. It's true. All your effort has come to nought. That exhaustion you carry deep in your bones is a clear signal to alter your self-improvement strategy away from dealing with the symptoms, to dealing with the core instead. But just because that's where it's showing up doesn't mean that's what's causing it. In fact, it's not what's causing it. It's never what's causing it.

Behaviour is just the end of the assembly line. It's just the end product out of the factory of your beliefs, your story, your fears, and what it is that you think is true about you and the world.

Upgrading your deep change strategy to version 2.0 means you focus on the:

- Core not the symptom
- Beliefs not the behaviour
- Story not strategy
- Fear not faith
- Seed not fruit
- Roots not leaves

Upgrade 3: Self-discipline to Self-permission

I've spoken at length about the difference between self-discipline and self-permission in my previous book *Elegantly Simple Solutions to Complex People Problems*, but it is such an important subject in the context of lasting change that it is important to revisit it here.

Self-permission

All lasting change comes through self-permission rather than self-discipline.

It is to take the handbrake off and allow yourself to be successful. It is to stop hiding your light under a basket and not conform to how the world wants you to be. It is the willingness to fully show up in the world in all your uniqueness and to shine for all to see. When you give yourself permission to flourish there is nothing strong enough or big enough to get in your way.

When you switch from the motivation of self-discipline to self-permission, everything changes. Self-discipline is motivation level 1.0. Self-permission is the 2.0 system upgrade. Instead of fighting against yourself you are now working with yourself. The self-improvement plan changes from imagining internal resistance must be overcome, to understanding all resistance must be understood and satisfied. This upgrade is about making peace with yourself, reconciling the past and moving forward as one. It's beautiful. It's long lasting and it makes much more sense.

When you make this upgrade, you get to take the handbrake off. Remember, it's like you are already sitting on top of the hill in a parked car, so when you take the brake off, there is no longer anything to hold you back. This is definitely a counter intuitive, counter-cultural system upgrade, but nevertheless it is a game changer.

This table highlights the key differences between both motivation strategies.

SELF DISCIPLINE	SELF PERMISSON
A behaviour management strategy. It only deals with the end product never the production line. Therefore, it will only produce short-term gains.	Focuses on changed beliefs which then automatically change the behaviour. It deals with the production line, not the end product.
A childish form of motivation. It requires no self-awareness or maturity and works only because you have energy to waste. It is the kindergarten version of trying to do your best work.	The adult form of motivation. As such, it allows you to access the best of who you really are and what you're capable of. It's an incredibly efficient and effective use of energy.
Based on the fear that you are weaker than you think.	Demonstrates that you are far stronger than you imagined.
Driven from the conscious mind. It pays no attention to the realm of the subconscious.	Accesses unconscious wisdom, intuition and knowing. It aligns your whole being to be pointed in the same direction.
Requires you to fight, dominate and control yourself to win. It feels like you must climb the snow-capped mountain to capture the flag.	Requires you to listen, trust, forgive, and accept yourself. It's releasing the handbrake to allow yourself to flourish and naturally move towards your goals.
Cruel and unnecessary. It ultimately violates your relationship with yourself and can lead to trauma.	It is 10 times more powerful and a sustainable form of motivation. It is a kind and loving way to access the best of you.
MASSIVLEY OVERRATED	**ALWAYS WINS**

©Jaemin Frazer 2019

Upgrade 4: Run away to Face up

The fourth aspect of the operating system upgrade is the strategy for dealing with life in all of its wonder and terror. Operating systems work so well because they take raw data and filter it through a predetermined set of criteria to avoid any ambiguity about what happens next. When this – then that. Easy. It may appear sometimes as if you are actually deciding what you will do, but the truth is the decision has already been made.

If you momentarily wrestle the power back and violate the system set up bad things happen like guilt, anxiety, and self-sabotage. It never works. Default settings are restored and patterns of behaviour continue.

The fourth upgrade is to apply Nathaniel Branden's psychology of self-esteem from practice one.

When life happens as it does, the good, the bad and the ugly, face up instead of running away. Operating system 1.0 for dealing with hard things is to run away. That ought to fix it. Upgrade 2.0 is to face up instead.

Typically, when hard things happen, it makes sense to avoid them because they're painful. Every cell in our body is designed to avoid pain and so when you don't know what to do, the best plan is to avoid it. Mask and medicate it. Run away from it. Yet in the process, every time we do run away, we don't escape scot-free. Branden's work helps unpack the fact that running actually undermines us. Because, in the process of running, we teach ourselves we don't have what it takes to deal with life, so we end up feeling terrible about ourselves and that we are not good enough.

Alternatively, facing up is much harder. Taking responsibility, confronting, owning, and dealing with stuff is hard, especially if you don't know what to do yet. Just the act of facing up, of being here, of turning the lights on, and being willing to deal with stuff in itself changes the game completely. Because it turns out you discover you're stronger than you think, and you do get through — you don't die. And in the process, you teach yourself that you've got what it takes to deal with life. One win leads to the next win and each win strengthens you and fills you full of confidence, strength and peace. You sleep well at night and you become enlarged. And that is the journey of transformation into who you really can be. Every time you run; you move further away from who you really could be. Every time you face up, well, you move closer to that ideal.

This part of the operating system upgrade totally changes your auto responses to dealing with the challenges of life.

- Instead of blaming others you take full responsibility.
- Instead of running away when things are hard, you face up.
- Instead of believing you are weak and fragile, you discover you are stronger than you thought.
- Instead of reinforcing the fear of inadequacy, you build success reference points.

Upgrade 5: Being the actor to Being the storyteller

The final part of the system upgrade revolves around who holds the pen. This is the sense-making part of the operating system.

Version 1.0 makes so much sense to understand that someone else has written the majority of your life. One or even multiple scriptwriters have cast you as the actor in their drama. You didn't ask to be included in the story and therefore, your life is the sum total of what everyone says to you and about you. You did not choose this. It is not your fault. It is what it is. All you can do is make the most of the cards you were dealt.

Upgrade 2.0 not only centres on you taking the pen back, but realising you are also the one dealing the cards (and no one is watching while you stack them in your favour). This seismic shift in worldview obviously changes everything. To fully buy the upgrade pack reveals the hidden truth that you don't just get the pen and cards now, you've actually always had them — it's all you. You are the only one with any real power in your life, so, what do you want? Who do you want to be? What are you prepared to do about it?

Who do you want to be?

You are not the actor you are the storyteller. Your life will clearly demonstrate the quality of the stories you tell. The cool thing is we constantly have the ability to upgrade the quality of our stories and improve them and deconstruct old ones and write new ones, more beautiful ones and more enlarging ones.

When people start the process of overcoming insecurity, the central question for many is — who am I? The further you travel down this path however, the more you discover that this question is impossible to answer. You initially go looking for how you've behaved in your past, what others have said about you and the results you've achieved. Yet, how could any of the data about who you really are be remotely accurate? It is simply the evidence of the story you've been living out of.

As abstract as it sounds, you really can be anyone you want to be. So the only appropriate question in discovering your identity is who do I want to be? Get clear on that answer and then go write the story until it becomes your reality.

Observing the real-life experience professional actors have of this concept is a great example. It proves not only that the story we live out of determines our experience of life, but that the story can be changed. Jim Carey gives a wonderful explanation of how this story telling works.

"I realized that I could lose myself in a character. I could live in a character. It was a choice. And when I finished with that, it took a month to remember who I was. 'What do I believe? What are my politics? What do I like and dislike?' It took me a while, and I was depressed going back into my concerns and my politics. But there was a shift that had already happened. And the shift was, 'Wait a second. If I can put Jim Carrey aside for four months, who is Jim Carrey? Who the hell is that?' ... I know now he does not really exist. He's ideas... Jim Carrey was an idea my parents gave me. Irish-Scottish-French was an idea I was given. Canadian was an idea that I was given. I had a hockey team and a religion and all of these things that cobble together into this kind of Frankenstein monster, this representation. It's like an avatar. These are all the things I am. You are not an actor, or a lawyer. No one is a lawyer. There are lawyers, law is practiced, but no one is a lawyer. There is no one, in fact, there."[17]

JIM CAREY

Everything is created twice

Of all the quality contributions Stephen Covey has made in the personal development space, I think perhaps his most important gift is the powerful observation that everything is created twice. He says that everything that exists has both a first creation in the unseen world (either by design or by default) and then the second creation is merely the manifestation of what has already

17   https://the-talks.com/interview/jim-carrey/

been created. This means that your current results are the ones you've already created for yourself whether you are aware of it or not. Therefore, if you want new results to show up in the real world, you have to go create them first in the unseen world.

After you have deconstructed old stories that are no longer serving you, holding yourself accountable as the storyteller with 100% choice and responsibility is the key to experiencing lasting change in your life. As the victim of someone else's story you have no power to change anything, but as the storyteller you are the one with the pen, so you are the one writing the scripts and you are the one with all the power!

Visualisation and affirmation

One of the most effective ways to do the work around designing new first creation results is through the technology of visualisation and affirmation. We bring things into existence by first seeing them, and then speaking them into being.

Sure, there are plenty of things in life we have no control over, but I'm sure most people have little idea of the creative power inside them for both good and evil. This lack of awareness often means they are already fully utilising the visualisation and affirmation technology against themselves instead of harnessing their own power to create positive things in their life. They focus and meditate on all the things they don't want to have happen and constantly talk about where they don't want to be.

Just imagining something in your mind or speaking some

words is *not* first creation work. However, when you picture yourself experiencing something and focus on this picture with enough energy to produce an associated feeling of resonance throughout your whole body then you are in the business of creating something new. The way this works is that if you can see it *and* feel it, you can have it. This applies to both positive and negative scenarios.

If you can see and feel yourself being lonely, sick or poor, you are creating that experience for your future self. If you can see and feel yourself being happily married, doing meaningful work and having an abundance of resources in the future then this is what you will see in the real world too.

Affirmations operate in exactly the same way. The way you talk to yourself and about yourself is again first creation work. If you can say it, and deeply agree with it, it will be true for you. As we've already explored, this applies to when you agree with both positive and negative things about yourself.

Be Do Have

I've explained the BE DO HAVE model in my previous book, but it has consistently been the go-to framework for me when I think about the work of effective storytelling in my life. Here are a few additional thoughts about how this model applies here. When you have an idea of the kind of results you'd like to see in your life, the only way to create them is to go and BE this person before you have any right to.

If your strategy is to focus on what you need to DO first, that puts you in the category of the worker — DO HAVE BE. The worker rationale is: The more I do, the more I'll have, the happier I'll be. The problem is, the more you do, the more there is still to do. The more you have, the more there is still to have. The BE-ing never comes.

If your strategy is to wait until someone or something recognises that you deserve these results and hands them to you, that positions you in the category of the victim. — HAVE DO BE. The victim rationale is: When I have been given what I need, then I'll do what needs to be done, and then I'll finally be happy. The problem is, life is unfair. Someone else has always been given more. The victim is always waiting on the world to change before they can start the work.

The only believable plan is to be the winner. That is to live by the model — BE DO HAVE. Don't start with what you need to DO, and never wait until you HAVE, just go BE. Then being the kind of person who has your desired results, start doing the kind of things that person would do, and then you will have the same results as them.

You don't write a best-selling book by waiting till someone opens the way for you and gives you all you need. Nor does anyone produce a best seller by just working really hard typing words. To genuinely succeed as an author, at some point you have to stop waiting and working and just go BE an author instead!

Until you can picture yourself and talk to/about yourself like you are this person already, no one else will ever see you this way either. Be the author first. Then do what the author would do. Then you'll experience what the author would have.

This book

I've had many stalled attempts trying to write this very book by falling into the trap of imagining it was just about working hard and getting it done. It was not until the 2020 global pandemic where business really slowed down and I had the chance to stop and ask myself what the gift was for me in this season. It became apparent that it was a beautiful opportunity to have the time and space to finish writing two books I had already started.

For the first two weeks of lockdown, I imagined this discovery would naturally lead to more book writing. However as hard as I tried, I felt no inspiration and my time kept being swallowed up by all kinds of other commitments and priorities.

The change came when I switched from thinking about what I needed to DO right now, to who I needed to BE. The clear rationale for this season was for me to be the artist and the writer. The moment I surrendered to that truth and fully entered into this way of being, the book flowed out of me. It also gave me the clarity to say no to everything else. If I'm being an artist and writer, then I'll go hide in a cave for the next however long until I emerge with a pair of finished books.

As I gave myself permission to go be the writer, it changed

the way I dressed, the food I ate, the time I went to bed and got up, and how much coffee and alcohol I drank. For two months I literally rotated between two outfits. I wore each for a week at a time, until a family member complained about my smell and then swapped for option B. I developed a bad case of dandruff as I was rarely styling my hair with product and so my scalp dried out. My office was littered with coffee cups and empty chip packets and I put on 5 kilos. But I could see and feel myself as a bestselling author the whole time, and as such, the books were born.

Agreements

A big part of my story telling ritual is reviewing my agreements. Don Miguel Ruiz says, it's our agreements that shape our whole experience of life. Interestingly, these agreements don't have to be negative and disempowering to get in the way.

Towards the end of 2019 my unconscious brought to the surface two historic agreements to be reviewed and updated. My piriformis muscle again grabbed my sciatic nerve over a period of two months to draw me into the need to have some very important conversations.

The first one was an agreement I made with Goulburn in my early 20's. As a passionate young man, desperate to do good in the world, I made an agreement that I was born in Goulburn and I would die in Goulburn. I would give every last ounce of blood, sweat and tears to this town and make whatever sacrifices necessary to make a difference here. While others would leave for greener pastures I would stay. One day I would even be the Mayor of Goulburn. As a young pastor, this agreement was beautiful and meaningful. It underpinned the story I was living out of in that season and helped me fully show up at my best.

However, seasons change. The trajectory of my life in this season is entirely incongruent with that agreement. My intention is to take my place as a global citizen, to have a big world experience and to one day consult to the UN on the subject of insecurity. My deep desire is to relocate to the eastern suburbs of Sydney and swim at Clovelly beach every day. However, as long as that old agreement is still intact, there is this weird guilt that pops up every time I talk of moving and an undercurrent of "hang on, what are you planning to do again? The UN? But you're from Goulburn." The old agreement tied my identity with my history and geography.

The most interesting part of this awareness was that it came within one week of moving into our dream house on the 20 acres only five minutes from Goulburn we'd always aimed for. The key message for me in this time was the importance of breaking up with Goulburn and changing my agreement about what was true for me.

This was my new agreement:

I am a global citizen. I have a global contribution to make. I will take my place among leaders, visionaries and change agents around the world and seek to increase the collective consciousness of the planet. Currently I lay my head to sleep in Goulburn. At the moment it serves my family's needs well and is a base from which to travel the world whenever is necessary.

The second agreement was another identity statement, but this one was made in my early 30's. As a way of exploring the full potential and power of my own physicality, I made a clear agreement that I was an athlete. I agreed that my body was fit and fast and that it was a machine capable of peak performance like I had never imagined possible. This agreement replaced a prior agreement made in year 8, where I decided I was the kid who tried harder than everyone else, but never won anything.

Off the back of this new agreement and identifying as an athlete I totally changed my performance ability. I shaved my legs, upgraded to a fancy carbon race bike and went and competed with the big boys. All my PB's and race wins came from this new agreement.

However, as I've already explained, this agreement meant the best of my ambitious energy always got directed to athletic goals. When I checked in with myself about how this agreement was impacting other areas of my life, the message was loud and clear.

I mean, congratulations Jaemin. You are the 2nd fastest runner at Goulburn Parkrun most weeks. While that is a truly wonderful achievement, no one really

214

cares. And in the context of Parkrun, anywhere the population is slightly larger; you would be lucky to be in the top 10. I understand how hard you've worked for this outstanding status amongst Goulburn's vast cohort of elite athletes, but, what if you were to divert your focus from that domain and invest all your ambitious energy into your entrepreneurial goals instead. Is it possible that you are sitting on something world class that is far more meaningful and important to give your life for?

The memo was to stop shaving my legs, break up with Strava and to no longer define myself as an athlete. This may seem like a small ask, yet it was a massive shift. To come to terms with the fact I had actually run all my PB's, would probably never run another marathon again, let alone ever achieve my goal of winning Townsville Marathon, and had in effect retired from competitive running, was a really big deal.

It was not that I couldn't run or ride anymore, it was just that these activities were now about giving energy to my entrepreneurial endeavours rather than taking energy away. The new agreement is now I am an entrepreneur with a global vision who enjoys running and riding as part of managing my state and replenishing energy.

To effectively be the storyteller in your life means regularly reviewing your agreements to make sure they are relevant and useful to your current life goals.

Rules and values

Another key aspect of the operating system upgrade also involves reviewing and improving the rules of the game.

It makes sense that we experience a sense of happiness and meaning in life when we live congruently with our values. Values are not only the things that are important to us, but they form the image of who we desire to be. As such, they are often formed as 'to be' statements rather than 'to do' or 'to have' statements in our mind.

- To be a good friend
- To be present for my family
- To be a good human
- To be generous
- To be fit and healthy
- To be a true Christian
- To make a difference to those around me
- To be a good husband/wife/father/mother/son/daughter/ brother/sister
- To reach my potential

The values list is probably fairly similar for most people. But where things differ greatly is the associated rules for each value. Whether you are aware of it or not, every value has some kind of internal measurement or standard. This rule is what informs you as to how effectively you are living out your values. The rule lets you know if you get a pass or fail — a tick or a cross on the score sheet.

When these hidden rules are observed and explored, they are often arbitrary and problematic. They are written by kinder-garteners making stuff up based on how they think the world works. As a result, these internal standards are almost never met! This leaves you feeling bad because now you are living incongruently with your values.

Is it important to you to be a healthy person? Great! But what's your rule about what is healthy and what is not? What is the standard? When do you get a tick? Exercise every day and eat zero added sugar? So, you miss one gym session and eat a bit of cake at your nephew's birthday party and now you are an unhealthy sluggard by your own standards!

You want to be present for your kids? Nice! But what does pres-ent mean? When do you actually get a tick here? Most of the time you are beating yourself up for not being present, feeling as though you are letting your kids down and as a result are a bad parent. So what's the standard? To be present means ALWAYS being there for your kids. Wait...Always? Yep. That's the rule. Always. Ok cool. Good luck with that.

Can you picture Parliament house filled with six-year-olds dressed up in suits passing bills and writing laws about this stuff? (It's probably not too dissimilar from what happens there normally, so it shouldn't be too much of a stretch). All these rules about how to be a good person, how to be a good parent, a good friend; what success, health, happiness etc. looks like, are all being constructed by a child.

- A good person never gets angry,
- A successful person has to earn over $1million,
- A healthy person must have a six-pack,
- A true Christian meets other people's needs before taking care of themselves,
- A good mother cooks dinner for her family every night,
- A good husband/father provides for all his family's financial needs.

More often than not, these rules are going to kick your arse and leave you feeling like you are NOT meeting your values. The problem is never the value. The problem is always the rule.

Successful people keep writing new and improved rules that keep the game moving forward. Think about the standards you'd like to create for yourself around each of your core values. You can make them as easy or as hard as you like! They are your rules. The point of this whole process is to remember that you, yes you, are the one with the pen. It has always been you. No one wrote these rules for you and you can change them as soon as you give yourself permission to.

What does a good person do?

How does a good person relate to friends, family, time, money?

What is right and wrong, good and bad?

Most people are still living out of rules they wrote as a child. No wonder things are messy as an adult!

Picture Harry and Marv from the Home Alone movies:

We're getting fooled by a kindygartener!

Write a story where it doesn't make sense to fail

Instead of writing stories that lock you out of growth and success, now is your chance to exercise the full power of your story-writing gift and create a script where failure is impossible. Remember, they are all works of fiction. You are not looking to tell true stories, just ones that work. How could you possibly know if they are true or not? You'll find evidence for whatever you believe is true.

Successful people tell better stories than those who struggle. They don't get stuck in or defined by any one story. They continue to update the script, develop their own character and keep taking the plot to ever more exciting and interesting places.

Here are some of the key components of successful story telling:

1.   Detach your identity from what you do

Cut off all external means of significance and replace them with internal ones. Take 100% ownership of your own value and worth. Your significance is not defined by what you do, or have, or what others think of you. Developing an internal sense of success and significance, instead of depending on what others think of you, means you can let go of driven-ness and come back to sustainable living; that is about adding value to yourself and others without being tied to or defined by what you do.

2. Pick yourself

American best-selling author and marketing guru, Seth Godin, says that too often people are waiting for someone else to pick them for the team. He says that the most important thing for people trying to make life work in today's world is to stop trying to get someone else to pick you and instead to go ahead and pick yourself. There has never been an easier time in the history of the world to; stand up, back yourself, create something beautiful and share it with the world. Stop waiting to be picked – it's time to pick yourself.[18]

3. Embrace uncertainty and back yourself

We cannot survive without certainty in our lives, but the most resourceful form of certainty is always to embrace the fact that there is no true certainty and back your own ability to step up and find a way when you need it most.

---

18   https://seths.blog/2015/03/pick-yourself-and-responsibility/

Updating the story

For the rewriting of the story to be effective therefore, it must include:

- A full operating system upgrade (downloaded AND installed. You'll need to reboot),
- Review, deconstruct and improve all past agreements,
- Review, deconstruct and improve all rules,
- Review, deconstruct and improve the script you are living out of,
- New first creation work.

Story State Strategy

Most people live their lives in this order: Strategy, State, Story. When they wake in the morning, the first thing they give attention to is action. The prevailing question occupying their mind is always; *What do I need to do?* They work from to-do lists and are constantly busy and lost in a sea of stuff to get done. They think success is entirely about how hard they can work, how much stuff they can get done and how disciplined and focused they are.

The problem is that the more you do, the more there is still to be done. There is no end point! Therefore, the constant experience is one of being behind. For the person stuck in this cycle of strategy-first living, they start each new day behind, overwhelmed and stressed. To make matters worse, all this strategy is done from whatever state they may find themselves in. Sometimes they are happy and full of energy, while other times they are flat and discouraged. They don't have any way of managing or controlling how they feel, and their state is affected by whatever is going on around them. The problem with this is the state you are in most determines the internal resources you have access to and therefore, the results you get. In a poor state, you produce poor results, no matter how hard you work.

Now behind all of this strategy and state is the story a person finds themselves in. The over-arching narrative they are living out of is the true limiter of their experience of life. The problem is that this story is often negative and disempowering and those who live strategy-state-story, often have zero awareness that they are actually living out of a story at all!

The Truman Show starring Jim Carey is a classic example of this. Truman thinks he's living his best life, when the truth is; his whole existence is controlled by a script, everyone in his world is a paid actor and he's living in a glass dome! No matter what he does, or how he feels, his experience is entirely governed by the story he is a part of.

Successful people who find a way to flourish and live unhindered from any limiting belief actually live their lives in the complete opposite way: Story, State, Strategy. Their first point of attention each new day is NOT to jump straight into action and strategy. They leave that till last. They understand that the real priority is to take care of the story they are living out of and so they always do this first.

Having done the work of deconstructing all limiting stories and writing new and expansive ones for themselves, they realign themselves to this story as their number one priority at the start of each new day. Using visualisations and affirmations, they remind themselves of who they really are and the kind of life they intend to live. At multiple points during the day, they anchor themselves back to this story again and again and again until it becomes the prevailing, dominating and default metanarrative of their life!

Having fully seen and experienced themselves as the kind of person they want to be, then they pay attention to managing their state. They practice life-giving rituals that affect every cell in their body and allow them to access a peak performance state and be at their absolute best when it matters most.

Finally, having taken care of story and state, they then go ahead and make a strategy about exactly what actions would be most effective and profitable in line with their most important goals and desires.

Story, state strategy. NOT Strategy, state story.

Therefore, Practice 7 brings all the preceding practices to completion. This final step allows you to genuinely solve the insecurity problem at your current level of growth so that you are free to move forward unhindered.

The trap with practice seven, is that many people want to rush straight to the end of the process without applying the preceding six practices.

> *Yep...Yeah...Yes...I've got it. I understand now. Thanks. Surely, I don't have to go digging back in my past to change this though? Can't I just focus on writing the new story now I know how this whole thing works?*

However, without fully deconstructing the old story first, re-writing your story becomes an exercise in behaviour management and self-discipline. As soon as you get tired, stressed or anxious, the old narrative will take over as your truth, like it always has.

The essence of practice 7 — Re-write the story:

Everything is created twice — Now is your chance to do new first creation work again. Be the storyteller not just the actor in the story. You are the one with the pen and paper giving meaning to your existence. Write the script for your life that gives you access to the future you desire.

Upgrade your operating system — Having dismantled the old system, now it's time to design a new operating system capable of handling the complexity of adult life. This system must include new agreements, rules and scripts.

Tell better stories — People who succeed in life just tell better stories. The point is not to focus on whether they are true or not, only if they are working for you.

Story, State, Strategy — NOT Strategy, State, Story. Get this right, and you'll have an unfair advantage in life. Align yourself to the new story every day as the first priority. This makes it the new default and prevailing metanarrative.

Own your value and worth internally — this is the journey of fully becoming an adult. That means replacing all the external ways you've met your core needs with internal ones. Overcoming insecurity is simply an issue of changing your own opinion of yourself. This is your work. No one else can do this for you.

Being Unhindered

Ultimately the aim of the game is to be able to show up to life unhindered by self-doubt, fear and limiting beliefs. This means we can be at our best where it matters most with nothing to prove or defend.

Solving the insecurity problem allows you to experience being fully unhindered on your current level of growth. However, being unhindered naturally leads to new levels of growth. If you are not held back by any internal limitations you inevitably will go beyond the boundaries of what has been safe, known and comfortable in exploration of new horizons. This growth then leads to new experiences of uncertainty and therefore exposes new levels of insecurity.

For example, someone who is secure about running a team of 3 staff, may be insecure about their capacity to lead 20 people and a person who is secure about their ability to earn $100k a year may be insecure about earning $250K. The point is that new insecurity shows up as evidence of growth not failure. It demonstrates true progress, not slipping back into old ways.

The metaphor matters

One of my clients experienced some significant frustration after our coaching relationship had ended because she kept describing her situation using 'onion language'. Every time she felt challenged by insecurity again, she saw it as evidence that she must have failed to get to the core of her limiting beliefs and therefore must go back to the very beginning to start the whole process again! Once she realised it was a new level of growth instead, and actually a new limiting belief revealed, she could face the new limiting belief revealed with better self-awareness, and without the frustration.

As she discovered, this process of overcoming insecurity is *not* like peeling layers of an onion at all. The onion metaphor suggests a linear process that happens once. Once you reach the core, you've reached perfection. You've made it! You'll never face another issue again! This misconception will only lead to delusion, frustration and disappointment.

I much prefer to imagine that we are spiralling up a never-ending mountain climb. We may experience the same issues each lap around the mountain, but each time we have gained altitude and are now experiencing the same issue from a different level.

It is crucial to realise that new experiences of insecurity represent growth and progress, not failure or regression. The framework you've just used to solve insecurity at this level of

227

growth will be the exact same 7 practices you'll use when you need them again.

> *"The solution to one problem is*
> *merely the creation of the next one."*
> MARK MANSON

It is important to accept that challenges will continue to come. A successful life is not absent of problems, but full of higher quality ones. Once you've sorted one issue there will always be another to take its place.

The more you embrace challenges rather than resisting them, the more quickly you grow through them. The more frequently you use this framework to solve insecurity as it arises, the more efficiently you'll move through each of the 7 essential practices each time.

Conclusion

So, there you have it! Without a doubt, personal insecurity is the biggest inhibitor of human performance and potential. While people are insecure about being insecure, it is just like almost every other problem in life. It has already been solved. The cool thing is, it's a predictable problem with a predictable solution. Therefore, all you need to overcome insecurity in your life is the proven framework and someone skilful enough to hold you in the space until it works. The aim of the game for adults is to become unhindered by doubt, fear and insecurity so that you are able to fully show up at your best where it matters most.

And just in case you're wondering...

Amanda — Apart from the occasional common head cold, Amanda is rarely sick. She has no need to be! She has found a way to have an adult relationship with her mum and gives herself permission to rest as part of her daily routine.

Robbie — Has not struggled with weight since giving himself full permission to be attractive. The extra weight no longer served a protective purpose in his life and as such, it dropped off him naturally and quite easily. He bought a whole new wardrobe and looks like a new man! As a bonus, he operates out of an entirely new level of confidence that has not only enhanced his health, but his business and his marriage as well.

Erica — She realised that this extra weight was evidence that she was hiding in every area of life, not just her marriage. She was afraid of showing up at her best for fear of being found out as inadequate. Over a 12-month period, Erica fully faced this fear and deconstructed the insecurity all the way back to the very first time she decided she was not pretty enough to fit in as a child. As she re-emerged, fully confident in her own opinion of her value and worth, it became apparent that her marriage would not survive. She had been pretending that things were ok for too long and was now no longer willing to tolerate the nature of their poor relationship. She is now a single mother of two running an award-winning successful business. As a result of the deep change work, she has also dropped 10 kilo's and is in love with how great she looks.

Bernadette – Is still obsessed with being skinny. The reward of being loved because of the way she looks is still too lucrative to let go of. This driven-ness continues to cause a range of other health and relationship issues in her life.

Jenny — Realised she needed to find safety and security in herself – not her husband. She accurately assessed her value and worth and fully owned it internally. This allowed her to show up to the marriage as the prize and to negotiate as an adult. As a result, her marriage is now stronger than it has ever been.

Mark – Has completely let go of the fear of rejection. I can still remember the breakthrough that came when he realised with joy that his whole experience with relationships had been created by the opinion of a four-year-old. It seemed so natural and easy to change the script from that moment. Mark is now enjoying new romantic relationships and the freedom to make friends wherever he goes.

Rachel – Is still single, but incredibly relaxed about it. She is totally focussed on loving herself. She knows full well that the only way a romantic relationship can work in the future is out of the overflow of a loving relationship with herself first. Rachel went back to the three-year-old girl with the painting and acknowledged that identifying with the jealous woman had served her for some time, but it was not the pattern she wanted for her future.

Christine – Although she was 3 standard deviations away from the average peak readiness for change, at 60 years of age, Christine proved that it was not too late. She examined her relationship with money and what it revealed about her relationship with herself, and decided to re-write the script she'd been living out of. Remarkably, she was then able to leverage her wealth of experience and accumulated assets to set herself up very well for retirement. Christine proved that she had given herself permission to flourish by not sabotaging her new financial plans and watching herself finally get ahead.

Geraldine – Stopped focussing on her bank balance and did the deep work around rebuilding trust with herself. She realised that her mother's controlling ways were simply a reflection of her own fear and insecurity and actually had nothing to do with her. Since then, off the back of deeply trusting herself, Geraldine had developed a very happy relationship with money, started her own business, and experienced the joy of her first long-term relationship.

Scott — Left the mines and started his own business doing what he had always dreamed of. Although being an entrepreneur has its challenges, he has never been happier and is incredibly grateful to have found the key to the golden handcuffs that kept him trapped for so long.

Rahini — Left her job and found a boss who couldn't live without her managerial skills. She worked there for five years, got every pay rise she asked for and then 'stuck it to the man' to become a consultant working for herself.

Trudy — Never finished the remaining coaching sessions we had booked together. I have since discovered that she did not solve the permission problem and has given up on her lifelong dream of writing a children's book. She has also gone back to working a job that she hates.